JN094856

English for Mass Communication

— 2024 Edition —

Hirofumi Horie
Kazuhisa Konishi
Shuji Miyazaki
Yasuko Uchino

ASAHI PRESS

音声再生アプリ「リスニング・トレーナー」を使った音声ダウンロード

朝日出版社開発のアプリ、「リスニング・トレーナー（リストレ）」を使えば、教科書の音声を
スマホ、タブレットに簡単にダウンロードできます。どうぞご活用ください。

◉ アプリ【リスニング・トレーナー】の使い方

《アプリのダウンロード》

App Store または Google Play から
「リスニング・トレーナー」のアプリ
（無料）をダウンロード

App Storeは
こちら▶

Google Playは
こちら▶

《アプリの使い方》

① アプリを開き「コンテンツを追加」をタップ
② 画面上部に【15714】を入力しDoneをタップ

音声ストリーミング配信 》》》

この教科書の音声は、
右記ウェブサイトにて
無料で配信しています。

https://text.asahipress.com/free/english/

記事提供：CNN / The Japan Times / NIKKEI ASIAN REVIEW / Reuters / Japan Times /
The New York Times / VOA News / The Wall Street Journal / 時事通信社 / 共同通信社 / The Guardian /
BBC / 読売新聞社

写真提供：CNN / iStock / アフロ / ロイター

表紙デザイン：大下賢一郎
本文イラスト：駿高泰子

English for Mass Communication — 2024 Edition —

Copyright ⓒ 2024 by Asahi Press
All rights reserved. No part of this publication may be reproduced in any form
without permission from the authors and the publisher.

は　し　が　き

　本書は、新聞・放送・オンラインで報じられる時事関連の英語ニュース（以下、「ニュース英語」）をできるだけ多角的に学べるように編集したものです。ニュース英語の学習は「ニュース英語を理解すること」、並びに「背景にある時事問題に関して英語でコミュニケーションすること」を目指します。

　学習の順序としては、いうまでもなく、「理解」から入っていかなければなりません。ニュース英語を読めず、音声で聞いてもよくわからない人が満足な英語を書いたり、話したりするとは期待できません。従って、本書の編集上の主眼は、「理解力の向上」となります。

　本書は、政治・経済・外交・軍事・環境からスポーツにいたる様々な分野の最新かつ主要な英語ニュースを理解していただくように編集してありますが、授業の組み立て方に沿って色々な使い方があると思います。例えば、最もオーソドックスな使い方としては、まずニュース英語の「理解力向上」に向けて二段階のアプローチを取ることです。第一段階ではニュース英語を「報道日本語」に移し替えて読解力を高めます。

　そして第二段階では、Exercise 1 の設問 1 でニュースの内容に関する英語で書かれた True/False Questions に答えることで、読解力のさらなる強化を図り、各ニュースの理解を深めます。設問 2 では、それぞれのニュースに含まれる Useful Expressions を用いてライティング練習をすることで、発信力の強化を目指します。

　Exercise 2 では異なる記事を用いて、再度ニュース英語の読解練習と、リスニング力強化に努めます。また、VOCABULARY BUILDUP で各章の関連語彙の習得を目指します。

　THE WORLD OF ENGLISH JOURNALISM は、ニュース英語の特質を理解するために重要な知識 15 項目を選別して、本書の後半部分に纏めてあります。適宜ご参照願い、英文ジャーナリズムに関する理解を深めて頂きたいと思います。

　なお、本書における英語の綴りや句読点は、原則として、オリジナル記事に準拠し、必要に応じて注を加えました（例えば、「アメリカ合衆国」の略称は通常、米国式では本文では U.S.、見出しでは US、英国式では本文、見出し共に US といった違いがあります）。また、ニュース記事の冒頭における発信地の明示についても、オリジナル記事に準拠しました。

　本書の内容を一層充実させるため、読者諸氏のご教示を頂ければ幸いです。

　最後に、本書の出版にあたり種々のお骨折りを頂いた朝日出版社の加藤愛理氏、田所メアリー氏にこの場を借りて厚く御礼申し上げます。

編　著　者

CONTENTS

THE WORLD OF ENGLISH JOURNALISM

Chapter 1

国内政治

「写真提供：共同通信社」

Before you read

ここに注目！

➤日本の国政のシステムは、日本国憲法に体現されている「国民主権」と「三権分立」が基本だ。特に立法府である国会で多数を維持する与党が行政府である内閣を形成する「議院内閣制」が政府の重要な骨格。

➤政党は、政権を獲得するため、選挙を通じ、国会でより多くの議席を得ようと、幅広い国民のニーズを捉える政策を掲げる。だが、近時は、政治スキャンダルなどが有権者に与えるイメージも大きな影響力を持つ。

➤急を告げる国際関係の影響もあって、安全保障問題のほか物価高などの経済問題など内外に課題は山積しており、難しい政策運営が求められている。

➤2021年9月以来政権を担ってきた岸田文雄総理は、世論を意識した政権維持に努めてきたものの、支持率の低迷に悩んできた。

➤こんな中、今までの政治スタイルに飽き足らない有権者の意向を先取りする日本維新の会など、従来型の与野党対立の構図を塗り替える動きも顕著になってきた。

➤これらの動きは、有権者にとって、より身近な地方政治の現場が発信元であることも大きな特徴だ。

➤Chapter 1では、こうした日本の国政や地方政治に関する動きが、どのように英語ニュースで伝えられているかを読み解いていこう。

NEWS 1

Ruling LDP faced unexpectedly close election battles

The ruling Liberal Democratic Party had unexpectedly close contests in Sunday's by-elections for Chiba Constituency No.5 in the House of Representatives and the Oita Constituency in the House of Councillors. And although the party secured victories in the lower house's Yamaguchi No.2 and No.4 constituencies, the LDP candidate was defeated in Wakayama Constituency No.1. 5

Prime Minister Fumio Kishida plans to analyze the outcome of the by-elections and carefully consider the timing for dissolving the lower house, while closely observing his Cabinet's approval rating.

"In the sense of a midterm assessment of the Kishida administration, the public gave us a favorable rating," LDP Secretary General Toshimitsu Motegi said to 10 reporters early Monday morning at party headquarters about the outcome of the by-elections. However, some LDP members expressed concern because an LDP-backed candidate was defeated in Wakayama and faced tough battles in other races.

The LDP camp initially seemed confident even as Nippon Ishin (Japan Innovation Party) gained momentum, winning the gubernatorial election in Nara 15 Prefecture in the first round of the unified local elections earlier this month.

An explosive was thrown at Kishida when he visited Wakayama Prefecture on April 15 to provide campaign support. The prime minister paid another visit on Saturday, but it did not help the LDP-backed candidate whip up support as expected.

In the lower house's Chiba Constituency No.5, where an LDP lawmaker 20 resigned over a political funds scandal, the LDP-backed candidate was expected to face headwinds. But opposition parties were unable to unite behind a single candidate, so the main opposition Constitutional Democratic Party and four other opposition parties ran separate contenders.

In Yamaguchi Constituency No.2, Nobuchiyo Kishi, the eldest son of former 25 Defense Minister Nobuo Kishi, won the seat held by his father. However, he faced backlash over the issue of hereditary succession after he posted a family history chart on his campaign website.

The LDP won four of the five by-elections, so an increasing number of LDP members will likely expect the prime minister to dissolve the lower house after the 30 May summit of the Group of Seven leading economies in Hiroshima. However, Kishida's tenure as LDP president does not end until September next year. If there is too long a period between the lower house election and the end of his presidential term, Kishida's approval rating may decline and there could be moves to unseat him as prime minister. People around Kishida have said he may dissolve the lower house 35 at the extraordinary Diet session in autumn after a Cabinet reshuffle.

— Based on a report on Japan News by the Yomiuri Shimbun on April 25, 2023 —

〈ニュース解説〉 2023年4月の統一地方選に合わせ実施された衆参5選挙区の補欠選挙で、自民党は4勝1敗としたものの、予想を超える接戦に苦しんだ。一方、この数年躍進を続ける日本維新の会は和歌山1区のほか、先に行われた奈良県知事選挙でも勝利するなど、党勢拡大が顕著となった。前年7月の参議院選挙を乗り切り、5月のG7広島サミット後の衆院解散も噂された岸田政権だったが、身内のスキャンダルや政策面の不手際等も加わり、先行きは不透明となった。

(Notes) 【※☞マークは *Useful Expressions*】

◆ **Ruling LDP faced unexpectedly close election battles** 「与党・自民党、予想外の接戦（に直面）衆参補欠選挙」[“LDP” は後掲 “Liberal Democratic Party（自由民主党）” の略語。“ruling party” は「与党」で “governing party” も同義。後掲 “opposition party”（野党）は反意語。“Elections” は、2023年4月に行われた衆参の補欠選挙を指す。☞ “close battle” は「（僅差で勝敗が決まる）接戦」「決戦」。ここでは、英語ニュースの見出し “headline” のスタイルに従い冠詞が省かれている。“headline” は、本記事のように冒頭段落の “lead” を要約する場合や記事内容から新たに書き下ろす場合がある。即時性と簡潔さを尊び、過去の事象にも現在形を用いる等、独特のスタイルがある。*P.88 “THE WORLD OF ENGLISH JOURNALISM（The headline）”* 参照]

◆ (L. 2) **by-elections** 補欠選挙（議員の辞職、死去等により欠員となった場合に実施される）

◆ (L. 2) **Chiba Constituency No.5 in the House of Representatives and the Oita Constituency in the House of Councillors** 衆議院千葉第5選挙区及び参議院大分選挙区 [英語ニュースでは、「衆議院」は後掲 “lower house（英国議会等の「下院」の意）” と、参議院は同 “upper house（「上院」）” と表現される場合が多い]

◆ (L. 4) **lower house's Yamaguchi No.2 and No.4 constituencies** 衆議院山口第2及び第4選挙区

◆ (L. 5) **Wakayama Constituency No.1** （衆議院）和歌山第1選挙区

◆ (L. 6) **Prime Minister Fumio Kishida** 岸田文雄首相（「首相」は「内閣総理大臣」の通称。単に「総理」とも呼ばれる。英語ニュースでは、“prime minister” の代わりに中国等で首相を表す “premier” も使われる）

◆ (L. 7) **dissolving the lower house** 衆議院解散

◆ (L. 8) **Cabinet's approval rating** 内閣支持率（メディア各社の世論調査による）

☞◆ (L. 9) **in the sense of** という意味では

◆ (L. 9) **a midterm assessment of the Kishida administration** 岸田政権の一つの中間評価

◆ (L. 10) **LDP Secretary General Toshimitsu Motegi** 茂木敏充自民党幹事長

◆ (L. 11) **party headquarters** 党本部

◆ (L. 14) **camp** 陣営（軍隊の野営地等の意味から派生し、志の同じ者の集まりを指す。“bloc” も同義）

◆ (L. 14) **Nippon Ishin (Japan Innovation Party)** 日本維新の会（自民党の活動に飽き足らない大阪の同党地方議員等が結成した地域政党「大阪維新の会」が国政に進出する際に創立。地方自治の拡大等をうたう憲法改正を主張する中道政党。“Japan Innovation Party” は以前の英語名）

◆ (L. 15) **the gubernatorial election in Nara Prefecture** 奈良県知事選挙（自民系分裂に乗じ維新候補が勝利）

◆ (L. 16) **the first round of the unified local elections** （2023年4月9日の）統一地方選挙前半戦

◆ (L. 17) **explosive** 爆発物（遊説中の岸田総理に手製爆発物が投げられた）

◆ (L. 20) **lawmaker** （国会）議員 [英語ニュースでは、国会の正式名称（後掲）“Diet” になじみのない読者のため、英国等で議会を意味する “Parliament” が多用され、国会議員も “Member of Parliament（MP）” の表現が使われる]

◆ (L. 21) **resigned over a political funds scandal** 政治資金スキャンダルで辞職した

☞◆ (L. 21) **LDP-backed candidate** 自民党公認候補（“LDP candidate 自民党候補” と同義。“-backed” は「〜に支援された、支持された」を意味する修飾語を作る用法）

☞◆ (L. 22) **headwind(s)** 逆風 [ここでは厳しい批判のたとえ。原義は「向かい風」。反意語は “tailwind（追い風）”]

◆ (L. 22) **unite behind a single candidate** 一本化した候補のもとで支持固めをする

◆ (L. 23) **the main opposition Constitutional Democratic Party of Japan** 主要野党の立憲民主党

◆ (L. 25) **Nobuchiyo Kishi** 岸信千代

◆ (L. 25) **former Defense Minister Nobuo Kishi** 岸信夫元防衛大臣（“former” は「元」、「前」両方を表すので文脈で判断）

◆ (L. 27) **backlash over the issue of hereditary succession** 世襲（アピール）問題に対する反発

◆ (L. 27) **family history chart** 家系図

◆ (L. 30-31) **the May summit of the Group of Seven leading economies in Hiroshima** 5月に広島で開催される先進7か国首脳会議 [Chapter4 News4（p.21）参照のこと]

◆ (L. 32) **Kishida's tenure as LDP president** 岸田氏の自民党総裁としての任期

◆ (L. 34-35) **unseat him as prime minister** 首相降ろし（退陣要求）

◆ (L. 36) **extraordinary Diet session** 臨時国会 [「通常国会（ordinary session）」以外に随時開催される。「特別国会（special session）」は衆院総選挙後に召集される]

◆ (L. 36) **a Cabinet reshuffle** 内閣改造（“a” は「あり得るもの」という不確定や可能性を表す用法）

1. 本文の内容と一致するものには T (True) を、一致しないものには F (False) を記せ。

(　　) (1) After close races, Prime Minister Kishida's LDP suffered crushing defeats in all the contested constituencies in the by-elections.

(　　) (2) With a victory in the elections, Kishida plans to dissolve the House of Representatives immediately, irrespective of his Cabinet's approval rating.

(　　) (3) LDP Secretary General Toshimitsu Motegi said that Kishida had gained voters' favorable rating in the sense of a midterm evaluation of his administration.

(　　) (4) Some Liberal Democrats are concerned about the party's prospects as an LDP-backed candidate was defeated in Wakayama and faced tough battles in other races.

(　　) (5) Nippon Ishin lost momentum, in spite of its victory in the gubernatorial election in Nara Prefecture in the first round of the unified local elections.

(　　) (6) The ruling Liberal Democratic Party won a perfect electoral victory over the five vacant seats in the Japanese parliament.

(　　) (7) In the lower house's Chiba Constituency No.5, the opposition camp failed to unite behind a single candidate and allowed the LDP-backed candidate to win the race.

(　　) (8) If there is too long a period between the next lower house election and the end of Kishida's tenure as LDP president, he might face a decline in his approval rating or moves to unseat him as prime minister.

2. 本文中に掲げた [*Useful Expressions*] を参照し、下記の語群を並び替えて空欄に適語を記し、日本語に合う英文を完成させよ。

(1) 国民の政治意識を測るバロメーターという意味で選挙における投票率を評価することができる。

Levels of voter turnout in elections can be evaluated (　　　) (　　　) (　　　) (　　　) (　　　) (　　　) that measures the political awareness of the people.

a	barometer	in	of	sense	the

(2) 一時は世界に名だたる電気製品メーカーだったその会社は、多大の逆風にもめげず更生を遂げた。

The company, which was once a world-famous manufacturer of electrical products, has managed to recover (　　　) (　　　) (　　　) (　　　) (　　　).

a	despite	headwind	lot	of

音声を聞き、下線部を補え。（２回録音されています。１回目はナチュラルスピード、２回目はスロースピードです。）

atural
4

Slow
6

Nippon Ishin stole the spotlight in local elections across Japan on Sunday, scoring decisive wins in its Osaka home base that [(1)] _____ _____ and is likely to impact its relationship on the national stage with the ruling Liberal Democratic Party and Komeito bloc.

Osaka incumbent Governor Hirofumi Yoshimura defeated his main rival, Mayumi Taniguchi, a political novice, while in the mayoral race, Hideyuki Yokoyama defeated Taeko Kitano, a former LDP Osaka city councilwoman. Both Taniguchi and Kitano [(2)] _____ . 　　5

In addition, Nippon Ishin won a majority of seats in both the prefectural and municipal assemblies for the first time, and its first-ever governor's seat outside of Osaka. 　　10

atural
5

Slow
7

Nippon Ishin's relationship with Komeito at the national level may soon change, too. In the Osaka City Council, Nippon Ishin's local party cooperated with Komeito to form the necessary majority [(3)] _____ _____ on two failed attempts to merge the city and the prefecture. 　　15

In return for that cooperation, Nippon Ishin [(4)] _____ _____ six Lower House districts in Osaka and Hyogo prefectures that were held by Komeito.

The central issue of the Osaka elections was [(5)] _____ _____, pushed hard by Nippon Ishin, to build an integrated 　　20 casino resort on Yumeshima, an artificial island in Osaka Bay that will also host the 2025 Osaka/Kansai Expo.

— Based on a report on Japantimes.co.jp on April 9, 2023 —

〈ニュース解説〉　大阪の地域政党をルーツに持つ日本維新の会。大阪都構想など独自の取り組みで注目を集めてきたが、ここ数年、同地域を超えた国政レベルでの活動を加速させ、従来型の政治スタイルに満足できない有権者の支持をバックに、野党最大勢力をうかがう伸張を見せている。2023年4月の統一地方選でも着実に歩を進め、与党・自公陣営の今後にも影響を与えそうだ。

(Notes)

stole the spotlight 注目をさらった　**local elections across Japan** 統一地方選挙　**decisive wins** 決定的な勝利　**Osaka home base** 本拠地大阪　**the national stage** 国政レベル　**Komeito** 公明党 **Osaka incumbent Governor Hirofumi Yoshimura** 現職の吉村洋文大阪府知事　**Mayumi Taniguchi** 谷口真由美　**a political novice** 新人政治家　**mayoral race**（大阪）市長選　**Hideyuki Yokoyama** 横山英幸　**Taeko Kitano** 北野妙子　**city councilwoman**（女性）市議　**a majority of seats in both the prefectural and municipal assemblies** 大阪府・市双方の議会での過半数　**first-ever governor's seat outside of Osaka**　大阪府以外で初の知事ポスト（奈良県知事を指す）　**Ishin's local party**（地域政党大阪維新の会を指す）　**merge the city and the prefecture** 大阪府と大阪市を統合する「大阪都」構想　**Osaka and Hyogo prefectures** 大阪府及び兵庫県（"prefecture" は「都道府県」を指すが、「東京都」は名称としては単に "Tokyo"、行政機関としては "Tokyo Metropolitan Government" と表記される）　**an integrated casino resort on Yumeshima** 夢洲統合型カジノリゾート　**artificial island** 人工島　**the 2025 Osaka/Kansai Expo** 2025年日本国際博覧会（公式略称「大阪・関西万博」）

■問A　空所 (a) ～ (n) にそれぞれ入るべき 1 語を下記の語群から選びその番号を記せ。

内閣府	→	Cabinet (a)
防衛省	→	Ministry of (b)
金融庁	→	Financial Services (c)
法務省	→	Ministry of (d)
総務省	→	Ministry of Internal Affairs and (e)
財務省	→	Ministry of (f)
外務省	→	Ministry of Foreign (g)
環境省	→	Ministry of the (h)
文部科学省	→	Ministry of (i), Culture, Sports, Science and Technology
厚生労働省	→	Ministry of (j), Labour, and Welfare
農林水産省	→	Ministry of Agriculture, Forestry and (k)
経済産業省	→	Ministry of Economy, (l) and Industry
国土交通省	→	Ministry of Land, (m), Transport and Tourism
国家公安委員会	→	National Public Safety (n)

1. Affairs	2. Agency	3. Commission
4. Communications	5. Defense	6. Education
7. Environment	8. Finance	9. Fisheries
10. Health	11. Infrastructure	12. Justice
13. Office	14. Trade	

■問B　(a) ～ (f) にそれぞれ対応する英語表現を下記の語群から選びその番号を記せ。

(a) 憲法　　(b) 国会　　(c) 総選挙　　(d) 与党　　(e) 野党　　(f) 連立

| 1. coalition | 2. constitution | 3. Diet |
| 4. general election | 5. opposition party | 6. ruling party |

■問C　(a) ～ (j) にそれぞれ入るべき 1 語を下記の語群から選びその番号を記せ。

自由民主党	→ (a) Democratic Party	立憲民主党	→ (b) Democratic Party of Jap
日本維新の会	→ Nippon (c) no Kai	公明党	→ (d) Party
国民民主党	→ Democratic Party for the (e)	日本共産党	→ Japanese (f) Party
小選挙区制	→ single-seat (g) system	比例代表制	→ proportional (h) system
衆議院	→ House of (i)	参議院	→ House of (j)

1. Communist	2. constituency	3. Constitutional	4. Councillors
5. Ishin	6. Komeito	7. Liberal	8. People
9. representation	10. Representatives		

Chapter 2

経済・ビジネス（1）

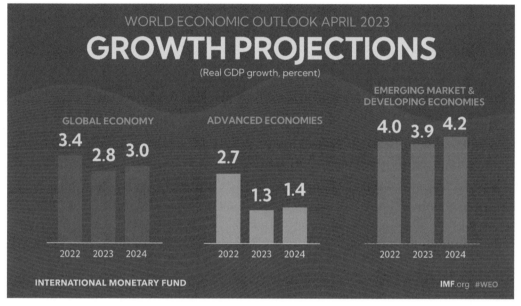

出典：国際通貨基金
https://www.imf.org/en/Publications/WEO/Issues/2023/04/11/world-economic-outlook-april-2023

Before you read

➤News 2 は、International Monetary Fund（国際通貨基金、略称：IMF）が 2023 年 4 月に発行した World Economic Outlook（世界経済見通し、略称 WEO）の主要点を報じている。WEO は各国政府に成長率の予測を示すと共に政策も提言し、経済運営や国際協調の重要な指針となる。

➤WEO は各国の経済成長率を積み上げて、Advanced Economies（先進国経済）、Emerging Market & Developing Economies（新興市場と発展途上国経済）、及び Global Economy（世界経済全体）の Real GDP growth（実質 GDP 成長率）を予測する。

➤2023 年 4 月時点の世界の実質 GDP 成長率は、2022 年が 3.4％と推計され、2023 年は 2.8％、2024 年は 3.0％と予測されている。こうした予測の背景には世界経済のどのような動きがあるのだろうか。

NEWS 2

Inflation tests a global economy that has weathered Covid-19, Ukraine war

WASHINGTON—The global economy has emerged from the pandemic and weathered the war in Ukraine with surprising resilience, policy makers gathered in Washington said last week. Yet the recovery remains fragile as stubborn inflation fuels risks in many corners of the world.

Top finance officials and central bankers patted each other on the back over the way their economies pulled through the past year, as they met for the spring meetings of the World Bank and the International Monetary Fund, their first fully in-person gathering in more than three years.

The global economy grew 3.4% last year even as the war upended energy and food trade. While this year's projected growth of 2.8% is hardly stellar, it is far better than in 2020, when the economy shrank by 2.8% amid pandemic lockdowns.

While cautioning about risks, Treasury Secretary Janet Yellen said the global economy looks better than people realize: "It's certainly stronger and brighter than last time we had the annual meetings in October." French finance minister Bruno Le Maire said the global outlook might be a bit rockier than expected, but "Europe is doing well."

Still, IMF and World Bank officials warned about what could go wrong in coming months. Inflation is persistent in the U.S. and in many countries, leaving the possibility that their central banks will continue raising interest rates.

Higher rates in the U.S., accompanied by a stronger dollar, could exacerbate the hardships of dozens of developing nations that have grappled with soaring costs of imported food and energy and faced ballooning debts. Commodity trade and external debts are often priced in dollars, making them sensitive to the Federal Reserve's policy changes.

Interest-rate increases could also reignite turmoil in the banking sector, which in March saw the failure of two midsize U.S. banks and the forced acquisition of Credit Suisse Group AG by its longtime rival UBS Group AG.

The IMF's baseline forecast for global growth is 2.8% in 2023. But it warns further financial stress could push that down to 2.5%, with advanced-economy growth falling below 1%. The multilateral lender said U.S. banking capacity will decline by 1% this year, shaving 0.44 percentage point off U.S. gross domestic product in 2023.

"Key is to monitor risks that may be hiding in the shadows in banks and nonbank financial institutions, or in sectors such as commercial real estate," said IMF Managing Director Kristalina Georgieva. "At this moment in time for the world economy, vigilance is absolutely paramount."

— Based on a report on The Wall Street Journal.com on April 16, 2023 —

〈ニュース解説〉 世界経済が新型コロナウイルス禍に見舞われたのが 2020 年で、実質 GDP 成長率は戦後最悪のマイナス 3.0％を記録した。21 年はワクチンの開発と先進国を中心とするワクチン接種の進展、各国の大型財政出動、先送りされた需要も取り込んだ経済活動の再開が奏功し、成長率は 6.0％と急回復した。但し、需要増と供給制約の影響でインフレ圧力が上昇に転じた。22 年に入ると、2 月にロシアがウクライナに侵攻。原油、天然ガス、小麦などの価格が暴騰し、世界的にインフレが加速。米欧で金融政策が引き締められ、中国の「ゼロコロナ」政策によるロックダウン（都市封鎖）の継続もあり、同年の成長率は 3.4％と推計されている。23 年は、多くの中央銀行がインフレ抑制を狙って、大規模な金融引き締めを継続すると見られ、成長率は 2.8％へ下降、24 年はインフレ率の引き下げを前提に、成長率は 3.0％へやや加速すると IMF は予測している。

(Notes) 【※☞マークは *Useful Expressions*】

◆ **inflation** インフレーション、インフレ（物価水準が全般的かつ持続的に上昇する現象）
◆ **Covid-19** Coronavirus disease of 2019 の略（本来は新型コロナウイルスが引き起こす感染症を指すが、新型コロナウイルス自体を意味することもある）
◆ **Ukraine War** ウクライナ戦争（2022 年 2 月のロシアによるウクライナ侵攻で始まった）
◆ (L. 2) **gathered** （自動詞の過去分詞を用いた分詞形容詞）
◆ (L. 5) **top finance officials and central bankers** （関係各国の）財務大臣と中央銀行総裁
◆ (L. 11) **pandemic lockdowns** 新型コロナウイルスの蔓延による都市封鎖
◆ (L. 12) **Treasury Secretary Janet Yellen** ジャネット・イエレン（米）財務長官
◆ (L. 13) **… looks better than people realize** （この than は元来接続詞であるが、ここでは関係代名詞的に使われている）
◆ (L. 14) **French finance minister Bruno Le Maire** ブリュノ・ル・メール仏経済・財務大臣
◆ (L. 17) **IMF** 国際通貨基金（International Monetary Fund）[1945 年に設立され、第 2 次世界大戦後の世界経済を支えてきた国際金融と為替相場の安定化を目指す国連の専門機関。2023 年 7 月現在の加盟国 190 か国。本部は米ワシントン D.C.。IMF は毎年 4 月と 10 月に "World Economic Outlook"（世界経済見通し：略称 WEO）を発行し、重要な変化がある場合は適宜、改定が加えられる。特に世界全体の動向を詳しく調べる特徴があり、各国の経済運営や国際協調の重要な指針となる]
◆ (L. 17) **World Bank** 世界銀行 [World Bank Group（世界銀行グループ）は 5 つの機関で構成される国連の専門機関。単に、World Bank と呼ぶ場合には 5 機関中、「国際復興開発銀行」（IBRD,1944 年設立）と「国際開発協会（IDA、1960 年設立）を指す。本部は米ワシントン D.C. で 2022 年 10 月時点の加盟国は 189 カ国。当初は大戦後のインフラ整備などに長期資金を提供する役割を担ったが時代とともに役割が変化。現在は、主に途上国向けの支援を中心に貧困削減などに取り組む]
◆ (L. 22) **ballooning debts** 急増する借入金、債務
◆ (L. 22) **commodity trade** 商品貿易（service trade は「サービス貿易」）
◆ (L. 22) **external debts** 対外債務
☞◆ (L. 23) **priced in dollars** ドル建て
◆ (L. 23) **Federal Reserve (Board)** 米連邦準備（制度）理事会（略称 FRB、米国の中央銀行で金融政策を通じて雇用の最大化と物価の安定を主な目標とする）
◆ (L. 25) **turmoil in the banking sector** 金融業界の混乱（which の先行詞は turmoil であることに注意）
☞◆ (L. 26) **saw** 「時」や「場所」を主語にして、「物事」や「状況」が「起こる」（happen）、「存在する」（exist）といった意味で使われる。
◆ (L. 26) **failure of two midsize U.S. banks** 米国の中堅銀行 2 行の経営破綻 [2 行とは Silicon Valley Bank（シリコンバレーバンク、本社：カリフォルニア）と Signature Bank（シグネチャー・バンク、本社：ニューヨーク）。前者はハイテク企業を主な取引先とし、コロナ禍の経済停滞・金融緩和下で預金の貸出先を十分に確保できず、余剰資金を主に国債で運用していた。しかし、米国のインフレ率が 2022 年に入って高騰する中、政策金利が同年 3 月以降大幅に引き上げられたため、銀行が保有する、より低利の国債は値下がりし、大きな含み損を抱えることとなった。その結果、不安に駆られた預金者による預金引き出しが急増し、経営破綻に至った。一方、後者は暗号資産（仮想通貨）関連業界との取引が中心だった。コロナ禍の中、同業界に流入した資金はインフレ高騰による金利高の中、引き上げられ、関連企業の経営が悪化、シグネチャー・バンクから預金引き出しが相次ぎ、経営破綻に繋がった]
◆ (L. 26) **forced acquisition** やむを得ぬ買収、（スイス政府が主導した）強制的な買収
◆ (L. 26) **Credit Suisse Group** クレディ・スイス・グループ AG（スイスに拠点を置く世界的な投資銀行。相次ぐ不祥事やリスク管理の甘さなどから業績が悪化し、2023 年 3 月に UBS グループとの合併に合意した。尚、AG は独語で「株式会社」の意味の略称。英語発音は「エイジー」）
◆ (L. 27) **UBS Group AG** UBS グループ AG（スイス最大の銀行）
◆ (L. 28) **baseline forecast** 標準見通し（各国の政策、金利、為替レート等、最も可能性が高いシナリオに基づく予測）
◆ (L. 29) **advanced-economy growth** 先進国経済の成長率
◆ (L. 30) **multilateral lender** 加盟国への（緊急）融資を行う機関（IMF を指す）
◆ (L. 31) **percentage point** （パーセンテージ）ポイント（例えば、5％と 10％の差は five percent ではなく、five percentage points）
◆ (L. 31) **gross domestic product** 国内総生産（GDP）
☞◆ (L. 33) **key is to …** 重要なことは…することだ（通常は The key is to …）
◆ (L. 33) **risks that may be hiding in shadows in …** …（の背後）に潜んでいる可能性がある（さまざまな）リスク
◆ (L. 34) **nonbank financial institutions** 銀行以外の金融機関（例えば、仮想通貨交換業、保険会社、ベンチャーキャピタルなど）
◆ (L. 34) **commercial real estate** 商業用不動産
◆ (L. 35) **IMF Managing Director Kristalina Georgieva** IMF 専務理事クリスタリナ・ゲオルギエヴァ

ニュースを読んで、下記の設問に答えよ。

1. 本文の内容と一致するものには T (True) を、一致しないものには F (False) を記せ。

(   ) (1) The global economy has successfully overcome the pandemic and the Ukraine War, suggesting the ongoing recovery will stay sound amid inflationary pressures.

(   ) (2) Participants in the World Bank and IMF meetings praised one another for their efforts in dealing with economic hardship during the past year.

(   ) (3) The global economy achieved an annual growth of 3.4% last year thanks to higher demand for energy and food generated by the war.

(   ) (4) Given U.S. Treasury Secretary Janet Yellen's statement on the global economy, it would be safe to say that she is cautiously optimistic about the current state of the global economy.

(   ) (5) IMF and World Bank officials warned about the possibility that the central banks' decision to continuously raise interest rates will result in persistent inflation.

2. 本文中に揚げた [*Useful Expressions*] を参照し、下記の語群を並び替えて空欄に適語を記し、日本語に合う英文を完成させよ。

(1) 日本企業が日本から輸出する場合には、ほとんどの契約が米ドル建てなので、円安は日本企業に有利だが、円高は不利となる。

When Japanese companies export from Japan, (   ) (   ) (   ) (   ) (   ) (   ); hence, a weak yen works to their advantage and a strong yen to their disadvantage.

are	contracts	in	most	priced	yen

(2) 近年、人工知能の分野で著しい進歩が見られ、以前には想定されなかった用途が開発されている。

The recent years (   ) (   ) (   ) (   ) (   ) the field of artificial intelligence, which have led to the development of applications that had never been thought possible.

advances	have	in	seen	spectacular

(3) 顧客に訴求力がある商品構成の重要性に触れて、最高経営責任者は鍵となるのは広範な選択肢とシンプルさとの間のバランスを取ることだと強調した。

Commenting on the importance of product assortment that appeals to customers, the CEO emphasized that (   ) (   ) (   ) (   ) (   ) a broad selection with simplicity.

balance	is	key	the	to

Natural
(10)

Slow
(12)

Inflation is beginning to abate meaningfully for American consumers. Gas is cheaper, eggs cost roughly half as much as they did in January, and prices are no longer climbing as rapidly across a wide array of products. But at least one person (1) _____ : Jerome H. Powell, the chair of the Federal Reserve.

5

The Fed has spent the past 15 months locked in an aggressive war against inflation, raising interest rates above 5 percent in an attempt to get price increases back down to a more normal pace. Last week, its officials announced that they were skipping a rate increase in June, (2) _____ how the already enacted changes are playing out across the economy.

10

Natural
(11)

Slow
(13)

But Mr. Powell emphasized that (3) _____ in the battle against rapid price increases. The reason: While less expensive gas and slower grocery price adjustments have helped overall inflation to fall from its four-decade peak last summer, food and fuel costs tend to jump around a lot. (4) _____ . And a measure of "core" inflation that strips out food and fuel is showing surprising staying power, as a range of purchases from dental care and hairstyling to education and car insurance continue to climb quickly in price.

15

Last week, Fed officials (5) _____ of how high core inflation would be at the end of 2023. They now see it at 3.9 percent, higher than the 3.6 percent they predicted in March and nearly twice their 2 percent inflation target. The economic picture, in short, is playing out on something of a split screen. While the steepest price increases appear to be over for consumers— a relief for many, and a development that President Biden and his advisers have celebrated—Fed policymakers and many outside economists see continued reasons for concern.

20

25

— Based on a report on nytimes.com on June 21, 2023 —

〈ニュース解説〉　米国金利の高騰は、News 2 が指摘するように米国経済のみならず、世界経済にとってもマイナスの影響を及ぼし得る。それにも拘わらず、米連邦準備理事会（FRB）は新型コロナウイルス禍に見舞われた米国経済を下支えするために 2020 年 3 月に導入した「ゼロ金利政策」を 22 年 3 月に解除し、更に 9 回の利上げを積み重ね、23 年 6 月時点の政策金利は 5.00-5.25％に達した。副作用があっても敢えてリスクを取る理由は、「消費大国」としてインフレの怖さを熟知しているからとされる。金融政策の効果発現には 12〜18 カ月程度のタイムラグがあると言われる。既に実施された利上げにより、2023 年末のコアインフレ率は 3.9％と予想されている（23 年 7 月時点）。FRB が目標とする 2％近辺を達成する道のりは、なお遠い。

(Notes)
meaningfully 明確に、はっきりと（ここでは、significantly と同義）　**Jerome H. Powell, the chair of the Federal Reserve** 米連邦準備理事会ジェローム・H・パウエル議長　**Fed** [**Federal Reserve Board** [米連邦準備（制度）理事会］の略称。邦字紙では初出は「米連邦準備理事会」とし、その後は「FRB」を用いるが、英文メディアでは Federal Reserve 又は Federal Reserve Board とし、その後は「Fed」を用いる］　**overall inflation** 総合インフレ率（「ヘッドライン・インフレ率」とも言い、物価全般の上昇率）　**"core" inflation** コアインフレ率［消費者物価指数（CPI）から短期的変動が激しい食品・エネルギーを除いたインフレ率で長期のトレンドを示すとされる。なお、日本では CPI から生鮮食品を除いたものを「コア CPI」、さらに「エネルギー」除いたものを「コアコア CPI」と呼ぶ］　**staying power** 持続力（「粘着度」、「粘着性」と訳されることもある）　**2 percent inflation target**（世界の多くの中央銀行が 1〜3％の範囲を健全なインフレ率とみているとされる）　**split screen** 分割スクリーン　**President Biden** 第 46 代米国大統領ジョー・バイデン［Joe Biden（Joseph Robinette Biden Jr.）］　**celebrate**（ここでは praise の意味）

■問A 空所 (a) 〜 (s) にそれぞれ入るべき1語を下記の語群から選びその番号を記せ。

国内総生産	→	(a) domestic product
消費者物価指数	→	(b) price index
卸売物価指数	→	(c) price index
非関税障壁	→	non-tariff (d)
最恵国	→	most (e) nation
政府開発援助	→	(f) development assistance
貿易不均衡	→	trade (g)
為替レート	→	(h) rate
国際収支	→	(i) of international payments
経常収支	→	current (j)
貿易自由化	→	trade (k)
社会保障	→	social (l)
企業の合併・買収	→	(m) and acquisition
株式公開買い付け	→	(n) bid
店頭取引株	→	over-the-(o) stock
優良株	→	(p) chip
不良債権	→	(q) loan
失業率	→	(r) rate
住宅着工件数	→	(s) starts

1. account	2. bad	3. balance	4. barrier
5. blue	6. consumer	7. counter	8. exchange
9. favored	10. gross	11. housing	12. imbalance
13. jobless	14. liberalization	15. merger	16. official
17. security	18. takeover	19. wholesale	

■問B (a) 〜 (d) をそれぞれ和訳せよ。

(a) European Central Bank

(b) Bank of Japan

(c) Federal Reserve Board

(d) New York Stock Exchange

■問C (a) 〜 (d) にそれぞれ対応する英語を下記の語群から選びその番号を記せ。

(a) 景気後退　　(b) 好況　　(c) 倒産　　(d) 年金

1. bankruptcy	2. bonus	3. boom	4. breakdown
5. pension	6. recession	7. rehabilitation	

Chapter 3

経済・ビジネス（2）

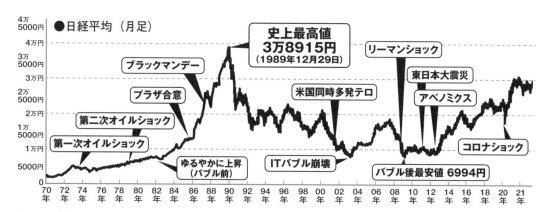

●日経平均（月足）

史上最高値 3万8915円（1989年12月29日）

- ブラックマンデー
- プラザ合意
- 第二次オイルショック
- 第一次オイルショック
- ゆるやかに上昇（バブル前）
- ITバブル崩壊
- 米国同時多発テロ
- リーマンショック
- 東日本大震災
- アベノミクス
- コロナショック
- バブル後最安値 6994円

➤バブル崩壊から今日に至る期間は、日本経済にとっての「失われた30年」と呼ばれる。
➤この期間には、株価や不動産価格の下落、金融機関の不良債権問題、企業倒産の増加、GDP成長率の低迷、デフレの進行、失業率の上昇、少子高齢化の進行といった問題が起こった。
➤2010年には日本の名目GDPはそれまでの世界第2位から米国、中国に次ぐ第3位となった。

「日米欧株価推移」（1979年〜2019年）

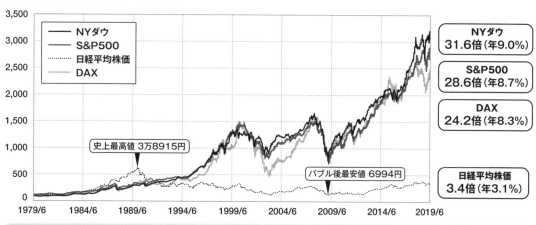

- NYダウ
- S&P500
- 日経平均株価
- DAX

史上最高値 3万8915円

バブル後最安値 6994円

NYダウ 31.6倍（年9.0%）

S&P500 28.6倍（年8.7%）

DAX 24.2倍（年8.3%）

日経平均株価 3.4倍（年3.1%）

➤上記は米、日、欧の株価指数の推移を1979年6月末を100として、その後40年間の変化を比較したもの。
➤日経平均が他3指標の値上がり率を上回ったのは大方、日本の資産バブルの頃。その後は大きく水をあけられているが、少子高齢化と移民が少ないことによる労働力不足が主たる要因とみるエコノミストもいる。
➤こうした背景を参考にして、News 3を読んでみよう。

NEWS 3

Disk 1
14
Japan's long-suffering stock market is back. This boom may have 'staying power'

Japan's stock market has waited more than three decades for its moment in the sun. The country's major stock indexes are trading at highs not seen since 1990, when its infamous asset bubble of the late 1980s was just deflating.

So far this year, the benchmark Topix has jumped almost 14%, and the Nikkei 225, which tracks Japan's blue-chip companies, has leapt nearly 17%. The indexes 5 have outpaced the United States' S&P 500 and Europe's Stoxx 600 benchmark indexes, which have both risen 8% in that time.

Investors say Japanese stocks have benefited from relatively cheap valuations, a long-awaited return of inflation, and a weakening currency. An endorsement by Warren Buffett undoubtedly played a significant role in the soaring prices of Japanese 10 stocks—the legendary investor told Japanese publication Nikkei in April that his flagship investment firm, Berkshire Hathaway, planned to increase its holdings in five Japanese companies. Foreign investors bought $15.6 billion worth of Japanese stocks last month, the highest monthly amount since October 2017, according to the Japan Exchange Group. 15

15
For years, investors have hoped modest rallies in Japanese stocks would translate into a sustained market revival for the world's third-largest economy, which is also home to a raft of household-name electronics companies and carmakers, like Sony and Toyota. But they never did. But this time, investors tell CNN, really is different.

Japanese stocks have received their biggest bump from an overhaul of corporate 20 governance rules that has compelled company executives to improve shareholder returns. JPMorgan analysts said last week that the "structural change" taking root in Japan could give the current market rally "staying power."

Earlier this year, the Tokyo Stock Exchange began telling companies to pay more attention to their stock price. It urged them to come up with plans to boost their 25 price-to-book (PTB) ratios—that is, the firm's share price relative to its net assets. Half of companies listed on the Tokyo Stock Exchange trade at a PTB ratio of less than one, according to Man Group data from February, compared with just 3% of firms on the S&P 500.

A low ratio means the stock is a bargain. The problem is that at least half of 30 Japan's companies have been stuck trading at a ratio of below one for most of the past 20 years. As a result, there has been little incentive for investors to buy the stocks if they don't believe they can sell them at a higher price later on.

— Based on a report on CNN.com on May 24, 2023 —

〈ニュース解説〉 日経平均株価が史上最高値である 3 万 8915 円を記録したのは、30 年以上前の 1989 年 12 月 29 日で、1986 年 11 月〜1991 年 5 月頃まで続いた「バブル景気」の末期であった。一国の株式指標はその国の経済のバロメーターともされることより、政府・日銀はバブル景気が崩壊した後、様々な景気対策を実施してきたが、日経平均株価は最高値には遠く及ばなかった。しかし、2021 年 2 月に至り、日経平均は一時、3 万円の大台を回復するなど、景気に漸く明るさが見え始めてきた。News 3 はこの辺の背景に焦点を当てている。

(Notes) 【※☞マークは *Useful Expressions*】
◆ **staying power** 持続力
◆ (L. 1) **(one's) moment in the sun** （特に、苦難を経て）注目を集める、成功する
◆ (L. 2) **stock index** 株価指数
◆ (L. 3) **asset bubble** 資産バブル（1986 年〜91 年頃に日本の不動産や株式などの資産は異常な高騰を見せた。主因は 1985 年の「プラザ合意」がもたらした「円高不況」への対策として政府・日銀が実施した金融・財政政策とされる。東京の山手線内側の土地を売却すれば米国全土が買えると言われ、日経平均株価も 1989 年 12 月 29 日に史上最高値 3 万 8915 円を付けた）
◆ (L. 4) **benchmark Topix** ベンチマークとして採用される東証株価指数 [「ベンチマーク」は本来、測量において利用する水準点を意味する。ベンチマーク指標は当該市場を代表する株価指数で、市場全体の相場動向を示す「物差し」の役割を果たす。TOPIX は Tokyo Stock Price Index の略で、2022 年 4 月まで東京証券取引所「市場第一部」に所属していた約 2200 銘柄で構成される。東京証券取引所（Tokyo Stock Exchange）は 22 年 4 月に市場区分を再編し、「市場第一部」、「市場第二部」といった区分は撤廃された。しかし、データの継続性を維持するために、旧「市場第一部」に属していた企業で構成される TOPIX が引き続き使用されている]
◆ (L. 4) **Nikkei 225** 日経平均株価、日経 225 種平均株価 [TOPIX を構成する約 2200 銘柄の内、取引が活発で流動性が高い 225 銘柄を日本経済新聞社が選定し、算出する。尚、本指数は日本の株式市場を代表するベンチマークだが、"tracks Japan's blue-chip companies" として紹介しているため、benchmark を省略して Nikkei 225 とのみ記載されている]
◆ (L. 5) **blue-chip companies** 優良企業
◆ (L. 6) **S&P 500** S&P500 種株価指数（米国の証券取引所に上場する代表的な 500 銘柄で構成。正式名：The Standard and Poor's 500）
◆ (L. 6) **Stoxx 600** STOXX600 欧州 600 指数（欧州先進国の証券取引所に上場する流動性が高い上位 600 銘柄で構成。正式名：The STOXX Europe 600 Index）
◆ (L. 8) **relatively cheap valuation** 相対的に割安な評価（第 6 段落の "price-to-book（PTB）ratios" に言及している）
◆ (L. 9) **return of inflation** インフレの再来
◆ (L. 9) **a weakening currency** 円安の進行（原義は「価値が減少する通貨」）
◆ (L. 9) **endorsement** お墨付き、認証
◆ (L. 10) **Warren Buffett** ウォーレン・バフェット [米国の著名投資家（1930 年生まれ）。2022 年 7 月時点の純資産 1167 億ドル（約 13 兆 4700 億円）で世界 7 位の富豪。20 年 8 月末、同氏が率いる米投資会社バークシャー・ハザウェイが、総額約 7 千億円で日本の大手総合商社 5 社の発行済み株式のそれぞれ 5%超を保有。最終的に比率を 9.9%まで増やす可能性があると述べた（23 年 6 月時点）。質素な生活で知られ、個人資産の 99%以上を慈善活動にあてると公言]
◆ (L. 11) **Japanese publication Nikkei** 日本経済新聞
◆ (L. 12) **flagship investment firm** 旗艦投資企業
◆ (L. 12) **holding** （通常複数形）保有資産（土地、株式等）
◆ (L. 13) **five Japanese companies** （ここでは、三菱商事を初めとする「5 大総合商社」を指している）
◆ (L. 13) **foreign investors** 海外投資家
◆ (L. 15) **Japan Exchange Group** 株式会社日本取引所グループ（東京証券取引所、大阪取引所といった取引所を運営する会社）
◆ (L. 17) **market revival** 相場の復活
◆ (L. 18) **Sony** ソニー株式会社（英：Sony Corporation）
◆ (L. 19) **Toyota** トヨタ自動車株式会社（英：Toyota Motor Corporation）
◆ (L. 19) **CNN** CNN（英：Cable News Network。本社：米ジョージア州アトランタ）
◆ (L. 20) **bump** 増加、値上がり（この文脈では "an increase in amount" の意）
◆ (L. 20-21) **overhaul of corporate governance rules** コーポレートガバナンス・コードの改訂 [「コーポレートガバナンス・コード」は金融庁と東京証券取引所により 2015 年に策定された。「取締役会などの責務」や「株主との対話」など 73 項目のガイドラインからなり、企業経営の透明性や効率性を高める狙いがある。18 年と 21 年に改定されているが、本ニュースにある "overhaul" は 23 年 1 月に東証が発表した、「株価純資産倍率」の引き上げに関するもの（次段落参照）]
◆ (L. 21-22) **improve shareholder returns** 株主への還元を拡充する（主に配当増や自社株買いによる）
◆ (L. 22) **JPMorgan** JP モルガン・チェース・アンド・カンパニー（英：JPMorgan Chase & Co.。米国最大の総合金融機関、本社：ニューヨーク]
◆ (L. 23) **market rally** 相場の上昇、急騰
☞◆ (L. 25) **come up with 〜** 〜思いつく、考案する
◆ (L. 26) **price-to-book (PTB) ratio** 株価純資産倍率 [通常、P/B ratio と略す。株価が 1 株あたりの純資産（総資産から負債を引いた金額で、企業の「清算価値」と同じ）の何倍かを示す。1 倍を割ると、清算価値を下回っており、割安、あるいは市場に評価されていないことになる]
◆ (L. 28) **Man Group** マン・グループ（英：Man Group plc。世界最古、最大級のヘッジファンド。本社：ロンドン）
☞◆ (L. 31) **be stuck 〈verb〉 +ing** （〈verb〉＋ing の状態に）追い込まれる（stuck の後に in や with を加えることもある）
☞◆ (L. 32) **incentive for 〜 to do …** 〜にとって…する動機、誘因

ニュースを読んで、下記の設問に答えよ。

1. 本文の内容と一致するものには T (True) を、一致しないものには F (False) を記せ。

(　　　) (1) The Japanese stock market has been lackluster for over 30 years since 1990, when sky-high asset prices began to plummet.

(　　　) (2) When Japan's major stock indexes climbed around 15% this year, they outshone America's S&P 500 and Europe's STOXX 600, which rose less than 10% respectively.

(　　　) (3) Nikkei reported in April that Berkshire Hathaway had plans to purchase more shares in five Japanese companies by spending $15.6 billion.

(　　　) (4) Sony and Toyota have failed to become a household name in their home market, because there are many other competing electronics and automobile makers there.

(　　　) (5) JPMorgan analysts viewed the recent trend in Japan of rewarding corporate shareholders more favorably was here to stay, indicating that the stock market may remain strong.

2. 本文中に揚げた［*Useful Expressions*］を参照し、下記の語群を並び替えて空欄に適語を記し、日本語に合う英文を完成させよ。

(1) その企業の経営陣は過去数年の経営不振を打開するために、斬新なビジネスのアイデアを創出しようと奮闘している。

The company's management is struggling to (　　　) (　　　) (　　　) (　　　) (　　　) (　　　) (　　　), in an effort to reverse the underperformance of the past few years.

> a　　business　　come　　idea　　novel　　up　　with

(2) その国の経済は、消費者が耐久財の購入を先延ばしにしており、需要の創出が不十分なため、デフレサイクルに陥っている。

The country has (　　　) (　　　) (　　　) (　　　) (　　　) a deflationary cycle, with consumers postponing the purchase of durable goods and creating inadequate demand.

> economy　　found　　in　　its　　stuck

(3) 多くの高給の仕事がデータの収集と分析能力を必要としているので、学生達はデジタル・リタラシーを身に着けることに増々インセンティブを感じている。

With many high-paying jobs requiring the skill to collect and analyze data, there is an increasing (　　　) (　　　) (　　　) (　　　) (　　　) (　　　) (　　　) digital literacy.

> equip　　for　　incentive　　students　　themselves　　to　　with

音声を聞き、下線部を補え。（２回録音されています。１回目はナチュラルスピード、２回目はスロースピードです。）

Natural **16**
Slow **18**

As Western central banks continue to jack up interest rates in an effort to douse stubbornly high inflation, China faces a growing risk of the opposite problem—deflation.

Prices charged by Chinese factories tumbled in May at their steepest annual pace in seven years, while consumer prices barely budged, ⁽¹⁾ _____ the world's second-largest economy both at home and abroad. 5

Economists say the absence of inflationary pressure means China ⁽²⁾ _____—a widespread fall in prices—if the economy doesn't pick up soon.

Natural **17**
Slow **19**

Persistent deflation tends to throttle growth and can be difficult to escape. 10 While a prolonged period of falling prices probably isn't in the cards, Chinese policy makers will nonetheless need to ⁽³⁾ _____ and get the economy motoring again, economists say, perhaps by trimming interest rates, weakening the currency, or offering cash or other spending inducements to households and businesses. 15

Ting Lu, chief China economist at Nomura in Hong Kong, said in a note to clients Friday that he expects local banks to cut key lending rates as soon as next week.

In remarks made at a meeting Wednesday and published by China's central bank after the release of monthly inflation data Friday, central-bank Gov. Yi Gang 20 said he ⁽⁴⁾ _____ in the second half of the year and exceed 1% in December. He said the People's Bank of China would use its tools to support the economy and promote employment.

Falling prices in China aren't necessarily bad news for the global economy, as lower costs to import Chinese goods should ⁽⁵⁾ _____ 25 that for many economies are still uncomfortably high.

— *Based on a report on The Wall Street Journal.com on June 12, 2023* —

〈ニュース解説〉 デフレ下では、物価が広範に下がり続ける。モノやサービスを安く買えるという利点はあるが、経済全体ではマイナスの影響が大きく、エコノミストの間では、デフレは経済をむしばみ、インフレ以上に対応が困難との見方で一致している。デフレ下で起こる悪循環を「デフレスパイラル」と呼ぶ。景気が悪化すると需要が減り、企業は値段を下げる。企業の利益が減ると、労働者の賃金が下がり消費が減る。さらにモノが売れなくなり、企業は投資や雇用を抑制し、景気はさらに悪化する。中国経済が不振な最大の要因は、住宅販売の落ち込みや新規開発の低迷が家電や家具などの耐久消費財、及び建材などの需要をも引き下げていることにある。関連業界を含めると中国の GDP の約３割を占めるとされる。

(Notes)
jack up 大幅に引き上げる　**douse** 抑制する（原義は「水をかけて鎮火する」）　**prices charged by Chinese factories**「生産者物価指数」を意味する［英：Producer Price Index（PPI）企業間で取引される原材料や製品の価格を指数化。日本では「企業間物価指数（CGPI：Corporate Goods Price Index）が用いられている］　**tumbled in May at their steepest annual pace in seven years** ５月に年率で過去７年に最も急激な下落を見せた　**consumer prices**「消費者物価指数」を意味する［英：Consumer Price Index（CPI）］を意味する　**deflation** デフレーション　**be in the cards** 可能性がある　**motor** 力強く稼働する　**perhaps**（ニュアンスとしては "possibly but not certainly" で "maybe" と同義）　**Ting Lu** ティン・ルー（Nomura International（Hong Kong）Ltd. の中国担当チーフ・エコノミスト）　**key lending rates** 主要貸出金利　**People's Bank of China** 中国人民銀行（中華人民共和国の中央銀行）

■問A 空所 (a) 〜 (s) にそれぞれ入るべき 1 語を下記の語群から選びその番号を記せ。

グローバル人材	→	globally (a) human resources
重厚長大産業	→	(b) industry
終身雇用	→	(c) employment
熟練労働者	→	(d) worker
年功序列昇進制度	→	(e)-based promotion system
能力主義昇進制度	→	(f)-based promotion system
食料自給率	→	food (g)-sufficiency rate
初任給	→	(h) salary
人材派遣会社	→	(i)-employment agency
数値目標	→	(j) target
正社員	→	(k) employee
契約社員	→	(l) employee
設備投資	→	(m) investment
先行指標	→	(n) indicator
遅行指標	→	(o) indicator
一致指標	→	(p) indicator
知的所有権	→	intellectual (q) rights
確定給付型年金	→	defined-(r) pension plan
確定拠出型年金	→	defined-(s) pension plan

1. benefit	2. capital	3. coincident	4. competitive
5. contract	6. contribution	7. full-time	8. lagging
9. leading	10. lifetime	11. numerical	12. performance
13. property	14. self	15. seniority	16. skilled
17. smokestack	18. starting	19. temporary	

■問B (a) 〜 (d) をそれぞれ和訳せよ。

(a) Asian Infrastructure Investment Bank
(b) Government Pension Investment Fund, Japan
(c) Japan External Trade Organization
(d) National Federation of Agricultural Cooperative Associations

■問C (a) 〜 (d) にそれぞれ対応する英語表現を下記の語群から選びその番号を記せ。

(a) 格安航空会社　　(b) 投資収益率　　(c) 有効求人倍率　　(d) 連結決算

1. consolidated earnings	2. effective labor force	3. low-cost carrier
4. ratio of job offers to seekers	5. return on investment	6. ultra-low airfare

外交・国際会議

「写真提供：画像上 共同通信社、
画像下 ZUMA Press／共同通信社」

Before you read

ここに注目！

➢ G7（Group of Seven）は西側先進国による、政治、経済、安全保障分野での広範な議題を討論する会議体。東西冷戦只中の 1975 年にフランスで開かれた G5 サミット（首脳会談）が始まり。冷戦終結後、ロシアも加わり G8 となったが、2014 年のクリミア侵攻によりロシアが離脱、自由民主主義先進工業国グループに回帰した。

➢ ロシアによるウクライナ侵攻により、権威主義的な国家への対応が一層重要な課題となり、EU（欧州連合）や軍事同盟である NATO（北大西洋条約機構）との連携強化の動きが鮮明となってきている。

➢ G7 と対比されるのが、2008 年のリーマンショックを契機に存在感を高めてきた G20（主要 20 か国）だ。だが、G20 には、G7 のほか、BRICS などの新興経済諸国（emerging economies）等が加わり、政治体制や立場の異なるメンバーもいることから、専ら経済問題に特化した議論を行っていることに注意したい。G20 サミットの正式呼称が「金融市場及び世界経済に関する首脳会議」であることは、その表れだ。ウクライナ問題、南・東シナ海での覇権主義的動きや人権問題など利害対立のある事項への実効的な共通認識を醸成することは困難であり、それが G20 の限界とされる。

➢ Chapter 4 では、国際情勢が変転する中、国際機関の動きや外交問題について、世界の英語ジャーナリズムがどのように報道しているか、2023 年 5 月に広島で開かれた G7 サミットや NATO 首脳会談に関するニュースを素材に、理解を深めていこう。

G7 communique amps up pressure on China, Russia

 HIROSHIMA, JAPAN—The Group of Seven industrial powers Saturday amplified its denunciation of China's rising military and economic security threats, while urging Beijing to press Russia to stop its military aggression and withdraw its troops from Ukraine.

In a communique of the G7 summit in Hiroshima, the group criticized China for ⁵ its use of "economic coercion," militarization of the South China Sea and "interference activities" aimed at undermining the safety of diplomats, the integrity of democratic institutions and economic prosperity.

Again, the G7 vowed to "support Ukraine for as long as it takes in the face of Russia's illegal war of aggression." ₁₀

The group said its approaches are not designed to harm China nor thwart its economic progress and development. It called on Beijing to engage with the G7 on climate, debt restructuring of vulnerable countries, global health and macroeconomic stability.

 "We are not decoupling or turning inwards," the communique said. "At the same ₁₅ time, we recognize that economic resilience requires de-risking and diversifying. We will take steps, individually and collectively, to invest in our own economic vibrancy. We will reduce excessive dependencies in our critical supply chains."

The group reiterated concerns about the situation in the East and South China Seas, and it encouraged Beijing to support a "comprehensive, just and lasting peace" ₂₀ in Ukraine.

The statement marks the strongest criticism of Beijing by the group since the 2021 G7 summit in Cornwall, U.K., when China was mentioned for the first time. The relatively mild language calling for a "peaceful solution" and opposing "unilateral attempts to change the status quo" in Taiwan, however, showed a compromise ₂₅ between G7 members—some of whom are uncomfortable about being too pointed on this issue, including French President Emmanuel Macron.

Earlier Saturday G7 leaders unveiled the "Coordination Platform on Economic Coercion," a new framework for countering the use of punitive trade practices for political goals. The framework is understood to target China without specifically ₃₀ naming the country.

Brazil, Comoros, Cook Islands, Indonesia, South Korea, Ukraine and Vietnam were invited by summit host Japanese Prime Minister Fumio Kishida as part of his outreach effort to the Global South. Kishida also invited prime ministers of India and Australia and convened them for the Quad meeting, which originally was scheduled ₃₅ early next week in Sydney but was preempted by negotiations in Washington to avoid a U.S. default and raise the country's debt ceiling.

— Based on a report on VOANews.com on May 20, 2023 —

〈ニュース解説〉 2023 年 5 月、G7 広島サミットが開催された。自らの出身選挙区である被爆地広島でサミットを開催し、核廃絶への道標にしたいとの岸田首相の強い意思が示された。2016 年の伊勢志摩サミットの際に安倍内閣（当時）の外務大臣としてオバマ米大統領（同）の広島訪問をアレンジした岸田氏は、ゼレンスキー・ウクライナ大統領やグローバル・サウスも含めた各国首脳の広島平和記念館訪問を実現させ、「核軍縮に関する広島首脳ビジョン」を発出するなど一定の成果を得た。今回も G7 の主要課題はロシアと中国だ。世界の安全保障と経済安定に向け、G7 の役割に注目が集まっている。

(Notes) 【※☞マークは *Useful Expressions*】

◆ **G7 communique amps up pressure on China, Russia** 「G7 コミュニケ　中国とロシアへの圧力を強める」［"G7 communique" G7 広島首脳コミュニケ（共同声明）（コミュニケは仏語 "communiqué" に由来）。"G7" は "Group of Seven（states, countries, nations, etc.）"の略称で「主要先進 7 か国」。その「首脳（Leaders）」による "Summit" は「頂上会談」の意。1975 年の G5（米日英仏独）首脳会合が初。後に伊及び加が参加し G7（先進 7 か国）に拡大。冷戦期にはソ連等東側に対抗する西側の政治・経済上の包括的会議体となった。ソ連崩壊後の 1991 年からゴルバチョフ大統領など歴代ロシア首脳が非公式に招待され、1998 年からは正式メンバーとなって G8 が成立した。だが、旧社会主義国ロシアは先進国とはみなされず、「主要 8 か国」と呼ばれた。2014 年、クリミア併合を理由に西側諸国が露主催のサミットをボイコット、G7 に戻った。議長国は毎年持ち回り。2023 年は日本の広島が開催地。"amp up pressure on" は「～への圧力を強める」。"amp" は後掲 "amplify（拡大する、増幅する）"の短縮形が由来］

◆ (L. 1) **industrial powers** 工業国家（"power" は「大国」のイメージ。軍事面も含めた「強国」を含意することもある。"economy" は経済面に着目した「国家」の意）

◆ (L. 2) **denunciation of China's rising military and economic security threats** 中国の軍事的台頭と経済安全保障上の脅威に対する非難

◆ (L. 3) **urging Beijing to press Russia to stop its military aggression and withdraw its troops from Ukraine** ウクライナへの軍事侵攻をやめ、軍を撤退させるようロシアに圧力をかけることを中国に強く働きかける［"Beijing" は中国（政府）を指す。首都名で当該国・政府を表す用法。☞ "urge … to ～ " は「～に…するよう強く働きかける、促す」］

◆ (L. 6) **economic coercion** 経済的威圧（経済的な脆弱性や依存関係を悪用する行為）

◆ (L. 6) **militarization of the South China Sea** 南シナ海の軍事化（同海域を中国の領海と主張、軍事基地を建設していること）

◆ (L. 6) **"interference activities" aimed at undermining the safety of diplomats, the integrity of democratic institutions and economic prosperity** 外交官の安全、民主的制度の健全性及び経済的繁栄を阻害することを狙った「干渉行動」

◆ (L. 9) **support Ukraine for as long as it takes in the face of Russia's illegal war of aggression** ロシアの違法な侵略戦争に直面するウクライナを、必要とされる限り支援する

◆ (L. 11) **not designed to harm China nor thwart its economic progress and development** 中国を害することを目的としておらず、中国の経済的進歩及び発展を妨げようともしていない

◆ (L. 12) **engage with the G7 on** ～という問題について G7 と連携して取り組む

◆ (L. 13) **climate, debt restructuring of vulnerable countries, global health and macroeconomic stability** 気候変動、脆弱国家の債務再編、世界的な保健衛生及びマクロ経済の安定

◆ (L. 15) **decoupling or turning inwards** デカップリング（切り離し）や内向き志向

◆ (L. 16) **economic resilience** 経済的強靭性（レジリエンス）

◆ (L. 16) **de-risking and diversifying** デリスキング（リスクの低減）と多様化

◆ (L. 18) **reduce excessive dependencies in our critical supply chains** 重要なサプライチェーンにおける過度な依存関係を低減する

◆ (L. 19) **East and South China Seas** 東シナ海及び南シナ海

◆ (L. 22) **the strongest criticism of Beijing by the group since the 2021 G7 summit in Cornwall, U.K.** 2021 年の英国コーンウォール・サミット以来 G7 による最も厳しい対中批判

◆ (L. 24) **relatively mild language calling for a "peaceful solution" and opposing "unilateral attempts to change the status quo" in Taiwan** 台湾に関して「平和的解決」を求め、「現状を変更する一方的な試みに」反対するという、比較的マイルドな表現［☞ "status quo" 現状、現状維持（ラテン語由来）］

◆ (L. 27) **French President Emmanuel Macron** エマニュエル・マクロン仏大統領

◆ (L. 28) **Coordination Platform on Economic Coercion** 経済的威圧に対する調整プラットフォーム

◆ (L. 30) **without specifically naming the country** 具体的国名は挙げない（特定国を名指ししない）

◆ (L. 32) **Brazil, Comoros, Cook Islands, Indonesia, South Korea, Ukraine and Vietnam** ブラジル、コモロ、クック諸島、インドネシア、韓国、ウクライナ及びベトナム

◆ (L. 34) **outreach effort to the Global South** グローバル・サウスへのアウトリーチ（手を差し伸べる）努力

◆ (L. 35) **convened them for the Quad meeting** クアッド会合を開催した［"Quad" は日米豪印による "Quadrilateral Security Dialogue（4 か国戦略対話）"の略称。安倍首相（当時）が提唱した "Free and Open Indo-Pacific（FOIP：自由で開かれたインド太平洋）構想 " を基に 2007 年成立］

◆ (L. 36) **was preempted by negotiations in Washington** ワシントンで行われる交渉が優先された

◆ (L. 36-37) **avoid a U.S. default and raise the country's debt ceiling** 米国の債務不履行を回避し、国の債務上限を引き上げる

1. 本文の内容と一致するものには T (True) を、一致しないものには F (False) を記せ。

(   ) (1) The Group of Seven wealthy nations weakened the tone of its denunciation of China's rising military and economic security threats, but strongly called on Beijing to press Moscow to stop Russia's military aggression and withdraw its troops from Ukraine.

(   ) (2) In the communique of the G7 summit in Hiroshima, the leaders criticized China for its use of economic coercion, militarization of the South China Sea and interference activities to undermine the safety of diplomats.

(   ) (3) G7 leaders reaffirmed their commitment to support Ukraine for as long as it takes in the face of Russia's illegal war.

(   ) (4) The G7 communique urged China to collaborate with the G7 countries to tackle climate change, debt restructuring of the poor world, and other issues of global significance.

(   ) (5) Having recognized de-risking and diversifying as essential for economic resilience, the G7 leaders stressed that they would seek to decouple with China and turn inwards.

(   ) (6) The relatively mild language in the communique calling for a peaceful solution and opposing unilateral attempts to change the status quo in Taiwan, was a result of a compromise with some of the countries, including France, who felt uncomfortable about being too harsh on this issue.

(   ) (7) Specifically naming China, G7 leaders announced the Coordination Platform on Economic Coercion, a new framework for countering the use of punitive trade practices for political goals.

2. 本文中に掲げた ［*Useful Expressions*］ を参照し、下記の語群を並び替えて空欄に適語を記し、日本語に合う英文を完成させよ。

(1) 地球温暖化の専門家は国際社会にカーボンニュートラル達成のための抜本的な努力を促している。

Global warming experts are (   ) (   ) (   ) (   ) (   ) make drastic efforts to achieve carbon neutrality.

> community   international   the   to   urging

(2) 大企業は現状維持志向が強いため、新ビジネスへの取り組みに出遅れがちだ。

Due to their strong desire (   ) (   ) (   ) (   ) (   ), large companies tend to lag behind in new business initiatives.

> maintain   quo   status   the   to

音声を聞き、下線部を補え。（２回録音されています。１回目はナチュラルスピード、２回目はスロースピードです。）

Natural 22 / Slow 24

NATO leaders said on Tuesday that Ukraine should be able to join the military alliance at some point in the future, but [(1)] _____ Kyiv an immediate invitation, angering Ukrainian President Volodymyr Zelenskyy.

The leaders were meeting at a summit in the Lithuanian capital of Vilnius as Ukrainian troops struggled to [(2)] _____ against the Russian invasion forces occupying parts of the country. 5

The leaders said in a declaration: "Ukraine's future is in NATO." But they offered no timeline for the process. "We will be in a position to extend an invitation to Ukraine to join the alliance [(3)] _____ ," the declaration said, without specifying the conditions Ukraine needs to meet. 10

Natural 23 / Slow 25

NATO did drop a requirement for Ukraine to fulfil what is called a Membership Action Plan (MAP), [(4)] _____ Kyiv's way into the alliance. Speaking at a rally in Vilnius on Tuesday, Zelenskyy voiced disappointment that Ukraine was not invited to join NATO. 15

NATO members in Eastern Europe have backed Kyiv's call, arguing that bringing Ukraine under NATO's [(5)] _____ Russia from attacking again. Countries such as the United States and Germany have been more cautious, wary of any move that they fear could draw NATO into a direct conflict with Russia. 20

— Based on a report on Reuters.com on July 12, 2023 —

〈ニュース解説〉　ロシアのウクライナ侵攻で、風雲急を告げる中、西側諸国の軍事同盟であるNATOの首脳会談が開催された。議題の中心は、ウクライナから示されたNATO加盟要請だ。ウクライナ支援には注力しつつ、ロシアとの直接紛争は避けたいNATOは、将来におけるウクライナの加盟に前向きな姿勢を見せつつも、加盟までのタイムラインを明示することは避けた。ゼレンスキー大統領はこの決定に不満を表しつつも、NATOの基本的な姿勢は評価しているとされる。

(Notes)

NATO leaders NATO（北大西洋条約機構）首脳　**the military alliance** 軍事同盟（NATOを指す）　**Kyiv** ウクライナを指す（原義は同国の首都キーウ。首都名で当該国を表す用法）　**Ukrainian President Volodymyr Zelenskyy** ウォロディミル・ゼレンスキー・ウクライナ大統領　**the Lithuanian capital Vilnius**（バルト三国の一つ）リトアニアの首都ヴィルニュス　**the Russian invasion forces** ロシアの侵攻軍　**declaration**（首脳）共同宣言　**timeline for the process** 加盟手続きに関する工程表（予定表）　**without specifying the conditions** 条件を明示することなく　**a Membership Action Plan (MAP)** 加盟行動計画　**Eastern Europe** 東欧（旧ソ連邦構成国やその同盟国。ウクライナも含まれる）　**could draw NATO into a direct conflict with Russia** NATOをロシアとの直接紛争に引き込む可能性（おそれ）がある

■問A　空所 (a) ～ (f) にそれぞれ入るべき 1 語を下記の語群から選びその番号を記せ。

国連総会（UNGA）　　　　　　　→　United Nations General (a)
国連安全保障理事会（UNSC）　　→　United Nations Security (b)
国連難民高等弁務官（UNHCR）　→　United Nations High (c) for Refugees
国連食糧農業機関（FAO）　　　　→　(United Nations) Food and Agriculture (d)
国際原子力機関（IAEA）　　　　 →　International Atomic Energy (e)
国際通貨基金（IMF）　　　　　　→　International Monetary (f)

> 1. Agency　　　2. Assembly　　　3. Commissioner　　　4. Council
> 5. Forum　　　6. Fund　　　7. Operation　　　8. Organization

■問B　(a) ～ (k) にそれぞれ入るべき 1 語を下記の語群から選びその番号を記せ。

国連教育科学文化機関（UNESCO）→　United Nations (a), Scientific and Cultural Organization
国際労働機関（ILO）　　　　　　→　International (b) Organization
世界保健機関（WHO）　　　　　　→　World (c) Organization
世界貿易機関（WTO）　　　　　　→　World (d) Organization
国際復興開発銀行（IBRD）　　　　→　International Bank for (e) and Development
アジア太平洋経済協力（APEC）　　→　Asia-Pacific (f) Cooperation
東南アジア諸国連合（ASEAN）　　→　(g) of Southeast Asian Nations
北大西洋条約機構（NATO）　　　　→　North Atlantic (h) Organization
石油輸出国機構（OPEC）　　　　　→　Organization of the (i) Exporting Countries
経済協力開発機構（OECD）　　　　→　Organisation for Economic (j) and Development
国際エネルギー機関（IEA）　　　　→　International (k) Agency

> 1. Association　　　2. Co-operation　　　3. Countries　　　4. Economic
> 5. Educational　　　6. Energy　　　7. Healing　　　8. Health
> 9. Labour　　　10. Leaders　　　11. Petroleum　　　12. Power
> 13. Reconstruction　　　14. Rehabilitation　　　15. Trade　　　16. Treaty

■問C　(a) ～ (g) をそれぞれ和訳せよ。

(a) Ambassador Extraordinary and Plenipotentiary
(b) diplomatic immunity
(c) ratification
(d) sovereignty
(e) COP
(f) exile
(g) economic sanctions

Chapter 5

軍事

Tsai Meets McCarthy　蔡英文・マッカーシー会談
「写真提供：共同通信社」

Before you read

笑顔で握手する蔡英文（ツァイ・インウェン）台湾総統とケヴィン・マッカーシー米国下院議長。経済支援の約束をちらつかせた中国の圧力で台湾と断交し中国と外交関係を結ぶ中南米諸国が増える中、中米で僅かに残った台湾承認国グアテマラとベリーズを訪問し、帰国途中に米国に立ち寄った蔡英文総統。1979 年の米中国交正常化以降、台湾の指導者が米国を正式訪問することは不可能になったが、写真にあるように他国訪問後の米国でのストップオーバーで米国政治の要人としばしば会談が行われる。もちろん中国は大反発。蔡・マッカーシー会談への対抗措置として、中国人民解放軍による台湾周辺海域や空域で大規模な軍事演習を実施した。Chapter 5 では、米中や台湾をめぐる微妙な関係を、世論調査結果にも注目して読んでみよう。

NEWS 5

Taiwan Voters Consider US-China Tensions

Disk 1

HONG KONG—When Taiwan's former and current presidents each embarked on overseas trips this month, their travels highlighted how rising tensions between the United States and China are seen by the islands' voters who will pick a new leader in January.

President Tsai Ing-wen met with U.S. House Speaker Kevin McCarthy and other 5 American legislators during stops in New York and California. Around the same time, Tsai's predecessor, former President Ma Ying-jeou, became the first Taiwanese former or current president to visit China since the two sides were separated at the end of the Chinese civil war in 1949.

Generally, Tsai's Democratic Progressive Party, founded in 1986, supports 10 Taiwanese nationalism and has championed building diplomatic ties with the U.S. and other nations. Ma's Kuomintang party generally favors building ties with Beijing as well as with the U.S. and other nations, and trying to find consensus.

Opinion polls conducted after the trips among Taiwanese adults 20 years and older found some 61% reported approving of Tsai's meeting with McCarthy while 15 22% disapproved. Ma's trip found opinions more evenly split, with some 39% of respondents saying they approved and 43% disapproving.

Tsai, her ruling Democratic Progressive Party known as the DPP, and their supporters see the meeting with McCarthy as an example of Taiwan's right to conduct diplomacy and an important step for Taiwan's security. 20

"In the face of pressure and intimidation, the people of Taiwan will only become more united," she said according to Taiwan's Central News Agency, adding that her meetings with the American legislators "will contribute to cross-Taiwan Strait stability and regional peace."

Former President Ma Ying-jeou remains influential after serving two terms in 25 office from 2008 to 2016 at a time when he improved relations with Beijing without losing Taiwan's self-rule, freedoms and democracy. On his "peace-building" mission this month, Ma told reporters, "the two sides must pursue peace, otherwise both sides will not have a future." While surveys indicated most Taiwanese support Tsai's U.S. visit, some voters worried that embracing Americans could further raise tensions with 30 China.

Washington adopted the "One China Policy" in 1979 when it switched diplomatic recognition from the Republic of China (Taiwan) to the mainland People's Republic of China. Under this policy, Washington acknowledges but does not accept Beijing's claim that Taiwan is a part of China to be reunified one day, preferring 35 that the two sides reach a peaceful resolution and urging both not to take unilateral actions that change the status quo. The One China Policy is not the same as the One China Principle, under which Beijing asserts Taiwan and the mainland are part of one country to be reunited one day.

— *Based on a report on VOANews.com on April 25, 2023* —

〈ニュース解説〉　2023 年 3 月 29 日、台湾の蔡英文（ツァイ・インウェン）総統は、訪問先の中米 2 か国（グアテマラとベリーズ）に向かう途中ニューヨークに到着し、支持者の歓迎を受けた。蔡総統の中米 2 か国訪問は、近年左翼政権が増え中国寄りの姿勢に傾く中南米諸国にあって台湾との同盟を維持する中米 2 か国を台湾支持に繋ぎとめておく意図があった。蔡総統は中米からの帰路も米国に立ち寄り、ケヴィン・マッカーシー下院議長と会談。この会談を中国は強く批判し、台湾近海での大規模軍事演習を実施した。

(Notes)　【※☞マークは *Useful Expressions*】

☞◆　(L. 1)　**embark on**　踏み出す、開始する、着手する

◆　(L. 2)　**highlight**　強調する、目立たせる

◆　(L. 5)　**President Tsai Ing-wen**　蔡英文総統（第 7 代台湾総統。初代総統は蒋介石。台湾独立を志向する民主進歩党の主席を 4 度務める）

◆　(L. 5)　**U.S. House Speaker Kevin McCarthy**　ケヴィン・マッカーシー米国下院議長［House は米国議会（Congress）の下院 the House of Representatives を指す。Speaker は下院議長のことで、米国大統領の死亡、辞任、執務不能の場合、大統領権限継承順位で副大統領兼上院議長に次いで第 2 位にある］

◆　(L. 7)　**former President Ma Ying-jeou**　馬英九前総統（第 6 代台湾総統。国民党主席を 2 度務める）

◆　(L. 9)　**Chinese civil war**　国共内戦［蒋介石の中国国民党と毛沢東が指導する中国共産党は日中戦争の間は一旦協力体制（第 2 次国共合作）を組んだが、1946 年 6 月から両者は全面的に対立。国民党は、1949 年には中国共産党指導下の中国人民解放軍に敗れ、台湾に撤退している］

◆　(L. 10)　**Democratic Progressive Party**　（台湾）民主進歩党［略語は DPP。日本語では民進党と略記されることが多い。党綱領で台湾共和国建設を掲げるも独立と現状維持の間を彷徨う。頼清徳（Lai Ching-Te 或いは William Lai）副総統が蔡英文の後継者として 2024 年 1 月の総統選挙の公認候補となっている］

◆　(L. 12)　**Kuomintang party**　国民党

◆　(L. 22)　**Taiwan's Central News Agency**　台湾中央通訊社（ちゅうおうつうしんしゃ。略称中央社。台湾唯一の国営通信社）

◆　(L. 23)　**cross-Taiwan Strait**　台湾海峡を挟んだ中国・台湾間の（台湾海峡は国際水域であり航行の自由が認められるが、中国政府は国際水域と見なしていない）

◆　(L. 26)　**Beijing**　中国政府（その国の首都の名でその国の政府や国全体を表す）

◆　(L. 27)　**self-rule**　自治

◆　(L. 32)　**Washington**　米国政府

◆　(L. 32)　**One China Policy**　一つの中国政策［この後に出てくる One China Principle「一つの中国原則」と区別。「1 つの中国原則」は中国政府が主張するもので、①世界で中国という名の下での主権国家はただ一つである、②中華人民共和国は中国を代表する唯一の合法政府である、③台湾は中国の不可分の一部である、の三原則が掲げられている。それに対し米国政府の立場である「一つの中国政策」は、②については承認する（recognize）が、①と③については、中国政府の立場を認知する（acknowledge）に留めている。台湾に対する米国政府の基本的立場は「戦略的両義性（strategic ambiguity）」と言えよう。

☞◆　(L. 36)　**unilateral**　一方的な［bilateral, trilateral, quadrilateral, multilateral と比較：bilateral は二国間の意味で、例えば bilateral trade agreement 二国間貿易協定。trilateral agreement としては米国、カナダ、メキシコ間の貿易協定である USMCA Agreement、quadrilateral agreement としては日米豪印 4 か国の戦略対話である Quadrilateral Security Dialogue、multilateral agreement としては、Trans-Pacific Partnership Agreement（TPP、環太平洋経済連携協定）がある］

1. 本文の内容と一致するものには T (True) を、一致しないものには F (False) を記せ。

( ) (1) It can easily be assumed that Taiwan President Tsai Ing-wen's stopover in the U.S. during her overseas trips was welcomed by the Chinese government.

( ) (2) The Kuomintang Party's Ma Ying-jeou was Taiwan's president immediately before Tsai Ing-wen took the same office.

( ) (3) The Kuomintang Party and the Democratic Progressive Party have been rival parties since 1949.

( ) (4) Compared with Kuomintang, the DPP tends to be more nationalistic and tries to maintain political distance from Beijing.

( ) (5) According to opinion polls, Tsai's meeting with U.S. Speaker of the House was received more favorably among the Taiwanese people than Ma's visit to Mainland China.

( ) (6) The news article seems to be supportive of the political stance taken by the Kuomintang Party rather than the one by the DPP.

( ) (7) The Kuomintang Party fully and unconditionally accepts the One China Principal claimed by the Chinese Communist government.

( ) (8) The U.S. government switches back and forth between the One China Policy and the One China Principal depending on the level of assertiveness of the Chinese government.

2. 本文中に掲げた下記の ［*Useful Expressions*］ を用いて空欄に適語を記し、日本語に合う英文を完成させよ。

(1) 〈 **embark on** 〉

The government should heed the warning and ( ).

政府は警告に耳を傾けて、根本的改革に着手すべきである。

(2) 〈 **unilateral** 〉

The French government may ( ) on border controls.

フランス政府は、出入国管理に関して一方的な措置を講じるかもしれない。

音声を聞き、下線部を補え。（２回録音されています。１回目はナチュラルスピード、２回目はスロースピードです。）

TOKYO—Japan, the U.K. and Italy aim to have a basic design for their jointly developed next-generation fighter by 2024 under plans discussed Thursday by the three nations' defense ministers.

The project, dubbed the Global Combat Air Program, will be [1] _____ among Japan's Mitsubishi Heavy Industries, 5 the U.K.'s BAE Systems and Italy's Leonardo.

It aims to [2] _____ state-of-the-art fifth-generation aircraft, such as the U.S.-made F-35.

Speaking at Thursday's meeting with Britain's Ben Wallace and Italy's Guido Crosetto, Japanese Defense Minister Yasukazu Hamada called the project "a 10 [3] _____ for generations to come."

As it weighed partners to develop a next-generation fighter jet, Tokyo chose, in 2020, to receive technical assistance from Lockheed Martin but later pivoted to the U.K. and Italy instead. This [4] _____ Japan's record of favoring American partners for joint defense programs. 15

Japan's Self-Defense Forces already use Lockheed's F-35 fighters. But many of the stealth jet's design aspects [5] _____ the Japanese side, limiting its ability to repair the jets at home.

— Based on a report on Nikkei Asia on March 17, 2023 —

〈ニュース解説〉　日本、英国、イタリアは 2035 年の配備を目途に、次期戦闘機（F-X）の共同開発計画「グローバル戦闘航空プログラム」に着手する。いわゆる第 6 世代戦闘機である。現在航空自衛隊は、米国の F-16 戦闘機を参考に日米共同で改造開発された F-2、双発でおそらく日本に一番必要な制空能力に優れた F-15「イーグル」と呼ばれる主力戦闘機、高いステルス性能を誇示する最新鋭の F-35A を装備するが、次期戦闘機では、防空任務に加え幅広い任務を担うマルチロール機を目指すことになりそうである。共同開発では、英国の BAE システムズ、日本の三菱重工業、イタリアのレオナルドが機体の設計・開発を担当する。日本が米国以外の国と戦闘機の共同開発に従事するのは初めてである。

(Notes)

the Global Combat Air Program（次期戦闘機共同開発計画である）グローバル戦闘航空プログラム
Mitsubishi Heavy Industries 三菱重工業　**BAE Systems** BAE システムズ（英国の国防・セキュリティ・航空宇宙関連の多国籍企業。前身のブリティッシュ・エアロスペースが組織改編された欧州最大の防衛関連企業である）　**Leonardo** レオナルド（イタリアの防衛・航空分野・安全保障関連企業）　**F-35** F-35 戦闘機（米国のステルス多用途戦闘機。第 5 世代ジェット戦闘機）　**Ben Wallace** ベン・ウォーレス（2019年 7 月より英国国防大臣。元軍人）　**Guido Crosetto** グイード・クロセット（イタリアの政治家、ビジネスマン。2022 年 10 月よりジョルジャ・メローニ政権で国防大臣を務める）　**Yasukazu Hamada** 浜田靖一（自民党衆議院議員。麻生内閣、岸田内閣で防衛大臣に就任）　**weigh** 量る、比較検討する　**Lockheed Martin** ロッキード・マーティン社（米国の航空機開発製造会社。F-22 や F-35 等のステルス戦闘機の開発及び製造で知られる）

■問A　自衛隊関連用語 (a) ～ (d) にそれぞれ入るべき 1 語を下記の語群から選びその番号を記せ。

自衛隊　　　　→　Japan Self-Defense (a)
陸上自衛隊　　→　Japan (b) Self-Defense Force
海上自衛隊　　→　Japan (c) Self-Defense Force
航空自衛隊　　→　Japan (d) Self-Defense Force

1. Air　　2. Force　　3. Forces　　4. Ground　　5. Maritime　　6. Sea

■問B　米軍関連用語 (a) ～ (e) をそれぞれ和訳せよ。

(a) United States Armed Forces
(b) United States Army
(c) United States Navy
(d) United States Air Force
(e) United States Marine Corps

■問C　軍事用語 (a) ～ (d) をそれぞれ和訳せよ。

(a) anti-ballistic missile (ABM)
(b) airborne warning and control system (AWACS)
(c) intermediate-range ballistic missile (IRBM)
(d) Nuclear Non-Proliferation Treaty (NPT)

■問D　(a) ～ (j) にそれぞれ対応する英語表現を下記の語群から選びその番号を記せ。

(a) 平和維持活動　　(b) 非武装地帯　　(c) 文民統制　　(d) 核軍縮
(e) 核保有国　　　　(f) 通常兵器　　　(g) 地雷　　　　(h) 休戦
(i) 大量破壊兵器　　(j) 自爆テロ

1. ceasefire
2. civilian control
3. conventional weapons
4. demilitarized zone (DMZ)
5. landmine
6. nuclear disarmament
7. nuclear powers
8. peacekeeping operations
9. terrorist suicide bombing
10. weapons of mass destruction (WMD)

Chapter 6

海外政治情勢

「新華社／共同通信イメージズ」

Before you read

ここに注目！

➤現在、世界には200を超える国や地域があるとされる。個々の生い立ち、歴史、そして現在の政治経済情勢は千差万別。だが、それらの実情を知り、理解することは、日本や私たち自身を知り、私たちの将来を考える上で大きな意味を持っている。その理解を助けるのが、英語ニュース。まず、知ることから始めよう。

➤Chapter 6のニュース、一つ目は、世界的には王室の数が少なくなってきた中、長い歴史と伝統を有する英国において70年ぶりに行われた王位継承について。チャールズ3世国王の戴冠式は、伝統と現代の融合を図る一大ページェント。王室の存在は英国の国際社会での立ち位置にも大きな影響力を持つ。経済的な課題を抱える中、王室に対する国民の意識も変化している。こうしたさまざまな事情を読みとろう。

➤さらに、議院内閣制など日本の国政制度の手本となった英国の政治システム、「君臨すれども統治せず」とされる英国王室と政治の関係などにも、理解を広げたい。

➤もう一つのニュースは、政府の債務上限をめぐる米国政治の動き。議会と大統領のユニークかつ緊張感を持った関係は、民主主義のもう一つの典型として私たちにも色々な示唆を与えてくれる。そして、4年に一度の米国大統領選挙にも注目しよう。

➤もちろん、欧米だけが世界ではない。アジア太平洋、中東、アフリカやラテンアメリカ、そして新興経済諸国や開発途上国など多様な国・地域がある。これらの政治・経済・社会・文化などについて、広範に知り、深く考える。そんなきっかけとしてもらいたい。

King Charles III crowned in ceremony blending history and change

Disk 1
32

LONDON—King Charles III was anointed and crowned on Saturday in Britain's biggest ceremonial event for seven decades, a display of pomp and pageantry that sought to marry 1,000 years of history with a monarchy fit for a new era.

In front of a congregation including about 100 world leaders and a television audience of millions, the Archbishop of Canterbury, the spiritual leader of the 5 Anglican Church, slowly placed the 360-year-old St Edward's Crown on Charles' head as he sat upon a 14th-century throne in Westminster Abbey.

With Britain struggling to find its way in the political maelstrom after its exit from the European Union and maintain its global standing, the monarchy's supporters say the royal family provides an international draw, a vital diplomatic tool and a 10 means of keeping it on the world stage.

"No other country could put on such a dazzling display—the processions, the pageantry, the ceremonies, and street parties," Prime Minister Rishi Sunak said. But despite Sunak's enthusiasm, the coronation took place amid a cost-of-living crisis and public scepticism, particularly among the young, about the role and relevance of the 15 monarchy.

Charles, 74, automatically succeeded his mother as king of the United Kingdom and 14 other realms, including Canada and Australia, when Queen Elizabeth died last September.

33

Saturday's event was on a smaller scale than that staged for her in 1953, but 20 still sought to be spectacular. There was an array of historical regalia from golden orbs and bejewelled swords to a sceptre holding the world's largest colourless cut diamond.

Charles looked solemn as he swore oaths to govern justly and uphold the Church of England, of which he is the titular head. He was then hidden from watching eyes 25 by a screen for the most sacred part of the ceremony when he was anointed on his hands, head and breast by Archbishop of Canterbury Justin Welby with holy oil consecrated in Jerusalem. After being presented with symbolic regalia, Welby placed the St Edward's Crown on his head and the congregation cried out "God save the King". 30

Gun salutes were fired at the Tower of London and across the capital, the nation, in Gibraltar, Bermuda, and on ships at sea.

After the service, Charles and Camilla, 75, departed in the four-tonne Gold State Coach built for George III, the last king of Britain's American colonies, to ride to Buckingham Palace in a one-mile procession of 4,000 military personnel from 39 35 nations. Tens of thousands of people ignored pouring rain to mass on the streets to watch what some saw as a moment of history.

— Based on a report on Reuters.com on May 6, 2023 —

〈ニュース解説〉 2022年9月に逝去された英国女王エリザベス2世の跡を継いで即位したチャールズ3世の戴冠式が、全世界数千万といわれる視聴者に向けビデオ中継される中、厳かに挙行された。前女王以来70年ぶりとなる伝統の儀式には、各国首脳等も参列。荘麗でありながら新時代の英国との融合を図る趣きも見られた。式後のパレードの沿道には大勢の国民が詰めかけた。だが、若い世代を中心に王室への支持には低下傾向がみられるほか、物価高騰や経済の低迷などブレグジット後の英国を取り巻く状況は厳しく、新国王の御代には先行きの不透明さも漂っている。

(Notes) 【※☞マークは *Useful Expressions*】

◆ **King Charles III crowned in ceremony blending history and change** 「チャールズ3世戴冠 歴史と変化を融合した式典」［”King Charles III (the Third)” ”チャールズ3世国王” 略称は “CIIIR：Charles III Rex (Rex はラテン語で王。女王は Regina)”。エリザベス2世の長男。2022年9月、女王の逝去とともに皇太子（Prince of Wales）から国王に即位。戴冠式は準備も必要なことから即位から時間をおいて実施された。“(be) crowned” 戴冠する。後掲 “coronation” も戴冠式の意。王冠のほか宝剣など王権の表章（regalia）が授けられ、王位継承の正統性が確認される。］
◆ (L. 1) **was anointed** 聖油を受ける［国王を神聖な存在として聖別（聖化）するための儀式］
◆ (L. 1) **Britain's biggest ceremonial event for seven decades** 英国にとり70年間で最大の儀礼
◆ (L. 2) **display of pomp and pageantry** 荘厳さと華麗さの展覧
◆ (L. 3) **sought to marry 1,000 years of history with a monarchy fit for a new era** 1000年の歴史（を持つ君主制）を新しい時代にふさわしい君主制と融合させようとする
◆ (L. 4) **in front of a congregation including about 100 world leaders and a television audience of millions** 約100人の世界の指導者を含む会衆と無数（何百万人も）のテレビ視聴者の前で
◆ (L. 5) **the Archbishop of Canterbury, the spiritual leader of the Anglican Church** 英国国教会の精神的指導者であるカンタベリー大主教
◆ (L. 6) **the 360-year-old St Edward's Crown** 制作後360年となるセント・エドワード懺悔王の王冠
◆ (L. 7) **a 14th-century throne in Westminster Abbey** ウェストミンスター寺院の14世紀に作られた玉座
◆ (L. 8) **find its way in the political maelstrom** 政治的混乱の中で英国の活路を見出す［☞ “find one's way” （苦労して）活路（進むべき道）を見出す］
◆ (L. 8) **its exit from the European Union** 欧州連合（EU）離脱［通称は “Brexit（Britain＋Exit）”］
◆ (L. 9) **maintain its global standing** 世界的な地位を維持する
◆ (L. 10) **the royal family** 王室
◆ (L. 10) **an international draw, a vital diplomatic tool and a means of keeping it on the world stage** 国際的な魅力、重要な外交ツール、英国（の地位）を世界の舞台で維持していく手段
◆ (L. 13) **Prime Minister Rishi Sunak** リシ・スナク首相（インド系移民の両親を持つ初の英国首相）
◆ (L. 14-16) **amid a cost-of-living crisis and public scepticism, particularly among the young, about the role and relevance of the monarchy** 生活費高騰の危機や、君主制の役割と妥当性について国民、特に若者が抱く懐疑の只中で（“scepticism” は英国式綴り。米国式は “skepticism”）
◆ (L. 17-18) **king of the United Kingdom and 14 other realms including Canada and Australia** 英（連合王）国のほか、カナダや豪州を含む14の（英連邦）諸国（Commonwealth realms）の国王
◆ (L. 18) **Queen Elizabeth** エリザベス（2世）女王（略称 EIIR：Elizabeth II Regina）
◆ (L. 21) **an array of historical regalia** 数多くの歴史的な宝物（レガリア、表章）
◆ (L. 21-23) **from golden orbs and bejewelled swords to a sceptre holding the world's largest colourless cut diamond** 黄金のオーブ（宝珠）や宝石をちりばめた剣から、世界最大の無色カットダイヤモンドが入った笏（しゃく）に至るまで（“bejewelled” ”sceptre” とも英国式綴り）
◆ (L. 24-25) **swore oaths to govern justly and uphold the Church of England - of which he is the titular head** 公正に統治し、名目上の首長である英国国教会を擁護することを誓った［☞ “swear (an) oath” 宣誓する］
◆ (L. 25-26) **hidden from watching eyes by a screen** スクリーンによって衆人環視から隠された
◆ (L. 26) **the most sacred part of the ceremony** 式典の最も神聖な部分
◆ (L. 27) **Justin Welby** ジャスティン・ウェルビー・カンタベリー大主教
◆ (L. 27-28) **holy oil consecrated in Jerusalem** エルサレムで聖別された聖油
◆ (L. 29-30) **"God save the King"** 「国王万歳！」（英国国歌の題名でもある。直訳は「神よ王を救い給え」。女王の場合 “King” は “Queen” に代わる）
◆ (L. 31) **gun salutes were fired** 祝砲（礼砲）がとどろいた（元首の場合は21発の空砲を撃つ）
◆ (L. 31-32) **the Tower of London and across the capital, the nation, in Gibraltar, Bermuda and on ships at sea** ロンドン塔から首都、全国、ジブラルタル、バミューダや海上艦船に至るまで
◆ (L. 33) **Camilla** カミラ王妃（王妃は正式には “Queen Consort” だが、実際には “Queen Camilla” と呼ばれる。君主である女王は “Queen Regnant”）
◆ (L. 33-34) **the four-tonne Gold State Coach** 4トンのゴールド・ステート・コーチ（馬車）（“tonne” は米国以外でのメトリック・トンの表記）
◆ (L. 34) **George III, the last king of Britain's American colonies** アメリカが英国植民地であった時代の最後の国王であるジョージ3世
◆ (L. 35) **Buckingham Palace** バッキンガム宮殿（ロンドン中心部の国王が最も常在する宮殿。そのほか国王は、ロンドン近郊のウィンザー城、スコットランドのバルモラル城、クリスマス時にはノーフォーク州のサンドリンガム・ハウスに滞在する）

ニュースを読んで、下記の設問に答えよ。

1. 本文の内容と一致するものには T (True) を、一致しないものには F (False) を記せ。

(   ) (1) King Charles III was anointed and crowned in one of the Britain's biggest ceremonial events in seven years.

(   ) (2) In front of a congregation including about 100 world leaders and a television audience of millions, the Archbishop of Canterbury placed the St Edward's Crown on Charles' head as he sat upon a throne in Westminster Abbey.

(   ) (3) With Britain struggling to find its way in the political turmoil after Brexit, opponents of the monarchy say the royal family provides an international draw, a vital diplomatic tool and a means of keeping it on the world stage.

(   ) (4) The coronation took place amid a cost-of-living crisis and public scepticism, particularly among the young, about the role and relevance of the monarchy.

(   ) (5) After being presented with symbolic regalia and the Crown being placed on Charles's head, the congregation cried out "God save the Queen."

(   ) (6) After the ceremony, Charles and Camilla departed in an open-top automobile to ride to Buckingham Palace in a one-mile procession of 4,000 military personnel.

(   ) (7) Gun salutes were fired not only at the Tower of London but also across the nation, and even in Gibraltar, Bermuda, and on ships at sea.

2. 本文中に掲げた［*Useful Expressions*］を参照し、下記の語群を並び替えて空欄に適語を記し、日本語に合う英文を完成させよ。

(1) 世界中で EV シフトが進む中、日本の自動車メーカーは将来に向けた自らの活路を見出すべく努力しなければならない。

As the world shifts to electric vehicles, Japanese automakers must strive (   ) (   ) (   ) (   ) (   ) (   ) the future.

| find | for | own | their | to | way |

(2) 就任式に臨み、当選した大統領は自らの職務を誠実に執行することを宣誓した。

At the inauguration ceremony, the newly-elected president (   ) (   ) (   ) (   ) (   ) his own duties.

| an | execute | faithfully | oath | swore | to |

音声を聞き、下線部を補え。（2回録音されています。1回目はナチュラルスピード、2回目はスロースピードです。）

Natural 34 / Slow 36

The U.S. Senate voted Thursday night 63-36 in support of a measure that will allow the United States to continue to pay its bills. The U.S. (1) _____ in four days. The bipartisan legislation now goes to President Joe Biden for his signature.

The House of Representatives overwhelmingly voted Wednesday night, with wide support from Republican and Democratic lawmakers alike, to allow the government to continue to borrow more money over the next year-and-a-half to (2) _____, exceeding the current $31.4 trillion debt limit.

Natural 35 / Slow 37

The legislation does not set a new monetary cap, but the borrowing authority would extend to January 2, 2025, two months past next year's presidential election. In addition, the legislation calls for maintaining (3) _____ _____ in the fiscal year starting in October, with a 1% increase in the following 12 months.

The House approved the legislation on a 314-117 vote despite objections by far-right Republican lawmakers who said it (4) _____ and from Democratic progressives who said it trimmed too much. Seventy-one lawmakers from the majority Republican party in the House voted against the bill, as did 46 Democrats.

The measure does not raise taxes, nor will it (5) _____ to increase, perhaps by another $3 trillion or more over the next year-and-a-half until the next expiration of the debt limit.

— *Based on a report on VOANews.com on June 1, 2023* —

〈ニュース解説〉 米連邦政府の国債発行上限額は、歳出関連法により 31.4 兆ドルと定められ、これを超えて資金調達はできない。このため、2023 年央には新規国債発行が不可能になると予想され、バイデン大統領と共和党のマッカーシー下院議長は上限撤廃につき協議を重ねてきた。交渉の末、超党派法案が上下両院で可決された。大統領署名を経て法律が成立すると、政府の支出可能額には制限が加わる一方、借り入れ限度が引き上げられ、デフォルト（債務不履行）は回避される。

(Notes)
U.S. Senate 米上院　**continue to pay its bills** 支出を続ける（"bill" は「請求書」の意）　**bipartisan legislation** 超党派の立法　**President Joe Biden** ジョー・バイデン米大統領　**signature** 署名（上下両院で可決された法案は大統領の署名により法律となる）　**House of Representatives** 米下院（後掲 "the House" も同義）　**Republican and Democratic lawmakers** 共和・民主両党の議員　**debt limit** 負債上限　**monetary cap** 借入額の上限　**borrowing authority** 借入権限　**fiscal year** 財政年度（米国政府の年度は 10 月から翌年 9 月末まで。米国企業の会計年度は自由裁量で、1 月〜12 月が多い）　**far-right** 極右の　**progressives** 進歩派　**raise taxes** 増税する　**expiration** 期限切れ

■問A 米国政府関連用語 (a) 〜 (i) にそれぞれ入るべき 1 語を下記の語群から選びその番号を記せ。

司法省	→	Department of (a)
財務省	→	Department of the (b)
内務省	→	Department of the (c)
国防総省	→	Department of (d)
中央情報局	→	Central (e) Agency
国家安全保障会議	→	National (f) Council
連邦捜査局	→	Federal Bureau of (g)
米国通商代表部	→	Office of the United States (h) Representative
国土安全保障省	→	Department of (i) Security

1. Defense　　2. Homeland　　3. Intelligence　　4. Interior　　5. Investigation
6. Justice　　7. Security　　8. Trade　　9. Treasury

■問B (a) 〜 (o) にそれぞれ対応する英文名称を下記の語群から選びその番号を記せ。

(a)（米）連邦議会　　　　(b)（米）下院　　　　(c)（米）上院
(d)（英）議会　　　　　　(e)（英）下院　　　　(f)（英）上院
(g)（米）民主党　　　　　(h)（米）共和党　　　(i)（英）自由民主党
(j)（英）労働党　　　　　(k)（英）保守党　　　(l)（米）国務長官
(m)（米）司法長官　　　　(n)（英）内相　　　　(o)（英）財務相（蔵相）

1. Attorney General　　　　　　2. Chancellor of the Exchequer
3. Congress　　　　　　　　　　4. Conservative Party
5. Democratic Party　　　　　　6. Home Secretary
7. House of Commons　　　　　　8. House of Lords
9. House of Representatives　　10. Labour Party
11. Liberal Democratic Party　　12. Parliament
13. Republican Party　　　　　　14. Secretary of State
15. Senate

■問C (a) 〜 (e) のアジア関連用語をそれぞれ和訳せよ。

(a) National People's Congress

(b) People's Liberation Army

(c) People's Daily

(d) Republic of Korea (ROK)

(e) Democratic People's Republic of Korea (DPRK)

Chapter 7

社会・文化

【日本における SNS の利用状況（個人）】

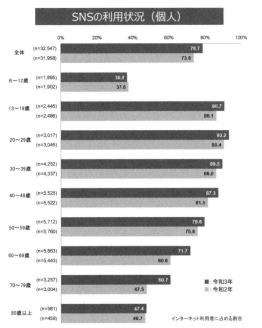

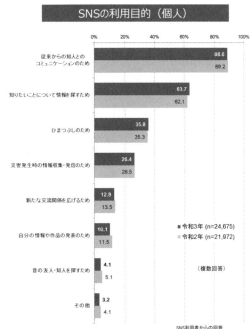

（令和 3 年通信利用動向調査の結果　総務省）

Before you read

SNS（Social Networking Service）や ITC（Information Technology Communication：情報通信技術）の普及により我々の社会・文化は大きく変化してきている。2022年（令和 4 年）に総務省が発表した「令和 3 年通信利用者動向調査」によると、回答者（3 万 2547 人）中 78.7 パーセントが Facebook、Twitter、LINE、mixi、Instagram、Skype などの SNS を利用している。若年層の利用度はさらに高く、この調査でも 13〜19 歳の回答者中 90.7 パーセントが SNS を利用していることが分かった。こうした中、若年層が被るネットいじめ等のリスクやメンタル面への悪影響が懸念されている。また、一方ではコロナ以降、ITC を有効活用した働き方変革も起こってきている。Chapter 7 では、これらの問題について考える。

Social media presents 'profound risk of harm' for kids, surgeon general says, calling attention to lack of research

There's not enough evidence to determine whether social media is safe enough for children and adolescents when it comes to their mental health, according to a new advisory from the US surgeon general.

Tuesday's advisory notes that although there are some benefits, social media use presents "a profound risk of harm" for kids. It calls for increased research into 5 social media's impact on youth mental health, as well as action from policymakers and technology companies. The 25-page advisory comes as a growing number of states are aiming to tighten regulations on social media platforms, including efforts in Montana to ban TikTok.

Surgeon general advisories are designed to call attention to urgent public health 10 issues and provide recommendations for how they should be addressed, the new report notes.

"We're in the middle of a youth mental health crisis, and I'm concerned that social media is contributing to the harm that kids are experiencing," Surgeon General Dr. Vivek Murthy told CNN. 15

"For too long, we have placed the entire burden of managing social media on the shoulders of parents and kids, despite the fact that these platforms are designed by some of the most talented engineers and designers in the world to maximize the amount of time that our kids spend on them," he said. "So that is not a fair fight. It's time for us to have the back of parents and kids." 20

The advisory includes a review of the available evidence on the effects of social media on youth mental health, noting that social media use among kids is "nearly universal." Up to 95% of kids ages 13 to 17 report using social media, with more than a third saying they use it "almost constantly." And although 13 is commonly the minimum age to use social media sites in the US, the advisory notes that nearly 40% 25 of kids ages 8 to 12 use the platforms, as well.

"We must acknowledge the growing body of research about potential harms, increase our collective understanding of the risks associated with social media use, and urgently take action to create safe and healthy digital environments," the advisory says. 30

— Based on a report on CNN.com on May 24, 2023 —

〈ニュース解説〉　SNS には、新しい友人ができる、友人や家族などとの既存のつながりが強まる、最新の情報やニュースを得られる、趣味や自分が興味のある話題についての情報が得られる、暇つぶしになるなど様々なメリットがあると言われる。一方、総務省情報通信白書（令和4年版）では、「SNS や動画配信サービス等の普及により、他人を誹謗中傷する表現や知的財産権侵害のコンテンツ等違法・有害情報や偽情報の拡散への懸念が増大」といった問題点も指摘されている。SNSを悪用した詐欺、ストーカーなどの犯罪行為、いじめなどのトラブルも多数報告されている。若年のSNS ユーザーが被る可能性のある不安やうつ状態など、メンタルヘルス面での問題も心配されている。

(Notes)　【※☞マークは *Useful Expressions*】

◆ **social media**　ソーシャルメディア［日本語では SNS（social media service）と表現される場合が多いが、英語では "social media" の表現が一般的］

◆ **surgeon general**　米公衆衛生局長官（医務総監と訳されることもある。米国の公衆衛生政策を統括する最高責任者で医師免許保有者が就任する）

◆ (L. 2)　**adolescent**　青少年［Cambridge Dictionary では "a young person who is developing into an adult"（成人になりつつある若年者）と定義されている。具体的には 13〜19 歳くらいの青少年を指す］

◆ (L. 3)　**advisory**　勧告書

◆ (L. 7)　**technology companies**　（SNS のプラットーフォームを運営している IT 企業を指す。プラットフォームとはサービスや商品を提供するための基盤や場を意味する）

◆ (L. 8-9)　**efforts in Montana to ban TikTok**　［米国西部モンタナ州は中国の ByteDance（字節跳動）社を親会社とする動画共有アプリ TikTok の事業を全面的に禁止する法律を 2023 年 5 月全米で初めて成立させた。同州知事によると、同法は「中国共産党から州民の個人情報を守るため」の措置であるが、同法には「TikTok は危険な行為を助長するコンテンツを未成年に提供した」とも記されている。米国では TikTok 利用者のデータが中国政府に渡るかも知れない懸念や中国が偽情報の拡散に TikTok を用いるかも知れない懸念から TikTok 規制強化論が高まっている］

◆ (L. 15)　**Dr. Vivek Murthy**　ヴィベック・マーシー博士

☞◆ (L. 16)　**for too long**　あまりにも長い間

◆ (L. 17)　**these platforms**　（Facebook, TikTok, WhatsUp, Instagram, Twitter 等の SNS のプラットフォームを指す）

◆ (L. 20)　**have the back of someone**　〜を支える、サポートする

☞◆ (L. 21)　**available**　（ものやサービスに関しては）利用可能な、（人間に関しては）手が空いている、都合がつく、時間がある

◆ (L. 22)　**…, noting that…**　（…and noted that…を意味する分詞構文。英語ニュースに頻出する構文）

◆ (L. 23-24)　**…, with more than a third saying…**　［with＋名詞句＋〜 ing（現在分詞）の形をとり付帯条件を示す。これも英語ニュースに頻出する構文］

◆ (L. 27)　**acknowledge the growing body of research about potential harms**　潜在的な危害に関して蓄積されてきている調査・研究結果を認識する［"acknowledge" は「重要性を認識する」、「了解する」、「感謝する」などを意味する多義語。

ニュースを読んで、下記の設問に答えよ。

1. 本文の内容と一致するものには T (True) を、一致しないものには F (False) を記せ。

(   ) (1) A new advisory from the US surgeon general emphasizes the need for conducting more research on the possible harms of social media on children and teenagers.

(   ) (2) Montana is the only state in the US that has been aiming to strengthen restrictions on social media sites.

(   ) (3) The surgeon general thinks social media can be seriously harmful to the mental health of young people.

(   ) (4) The US government has so far strongly supported parents to reduce possible risks of social media on their children.

(   ) (5) Kids under 13 years old can never use social media in the US.

2. 本文中に掲げた［*Useful Expressions*］を参照し、下記の語群を並び替えて空欄に適語を記し、日本語に合う英文を完成させよ。

(1) あなたは長く話しすぎたので、このあたりでストップしていただけますか？

You (   ) (   ) (   ) (   ) (   ), (   ) could you (   ) (   )?

> for,   have,   here,   long,   so,   stop,   talked,   too

(2) 明日面接をする時間はありそうですか？

Do (   ) (   ) you will (   ) (   ) (   ) an (   ) tomorrow?

> available,   be,   for,   interview,   think,   you

音声を聞き、下線部を補え。（2回録音されています。1回目はナチュラルスピード、2回目はスロースピードです。）

Natural 40 **Slow** 42

Japanese companies are divided over whether to keep remote working arrangements in place after the country downgrades COVID-19 to a lower-risk (1) _____ on Monday.

Some major companies have been shifting back to (2) _____. Others are cautious about fully returning to the office-based work style. 5

A survey conducted by Teikoku Databank Ltd., a research company, in March showed about 40% of 11,428 (3) _____ said they will return to pre-pandemic ways of working once the status of COVID-19 is lowered.

Natural 41 **Slow** 43

Almost (4) _____ with work styles introduced during the pandemic. Among companies with over 1,000 employees, those planning to maintain pandemic-era work styles accounted for over 50%. 10

In April last year, Honda Motor Co. shifted its focus back to face-to-face working at all of its departments. "In the manufacturing industry, having face-to-face conversations while actually looking at products is important," a public relations official said. 15

(5) _____, regardless of working at the office or from home," said an official of electronics maker NEC Corp. The share of NEC workers coming to the office has been at around 30% to 40% and the company plans to maintain remote working arrangements.

— *Based on The Japan News on Jiji Press on May 7, 2023* —

〈ニュース解説〉　新型コロナウイルスの感染でリモートワークは日本企業にも浸透したかのように見えた。しかし、コロナの感染症法上の位置づけが 2023 年 5 月にそれまでの 2 類から季節性インフルエンザなどと同じ 5 類に移行するのに先立ち、その後の働き方に関して帝国データバンクが実施した調査では、企業により対応ぶりが様々であることが判明した。この調査では、「コロナ前とは働き方が異なる」と回答した企業は 38 パーセントだった一方、「コロナ前と同じ」と回答した企業も 39 パーセントにのぼった。「コロナ前と同じ」との回答は業種別では農林水産、建設、不動産、金融、製造に多かった。また、「コロナ前とは異なる」との回答は従業員規模の大きな企業に多かった。

(Notes)

downgrade COVID-19 to a lower risk category（コロナの感染症法上の分類を 2 類から 5 類に移行することを意味する。2 類とは感染力や罹患した場合の重篤性から危険度が高いとされる感染症）　**Teikoku Data Bank (Ltd.)**　株式会社帝国データバンク（大手の民間信用調査会社）　**Honda Motor Co.** 本田技研工業株式会社（通称ホンダ）　**public relations official** 広報責任者、広報担当幹部社員（Cambridge Dictionary は "official" を "a person who has a position of responsibility in an organization" と定義している。企業の場合には幹部社員、責任者といった意味。企業の役員は executive, officer, director などと表現される）　**NEC Corp.** 日本電気株式会社（日本語でも通称 NEC）

■問A　空所 (a) ～ (j) にそれぞれ入るべき 1 語を下記の語群から選びその番号を記せ。

体罰	→	(a) punishment
帰国子女	→	(b) children
ひきこもり	→	social (c)
ネットいじめ	→	cyber (d)
学級崩壊	→	classroom (e)
適応障害	→	(f) disorder
性同一性障害	→	(g) identity disorder
核家族	→	(h) family
出産休暇（産休）	→	maternity (i)
共働き世帯	→	(j)-earner household

1. adjustment　　2. bullying　　3. corporal　　4. disintegration
5. dual　　6. gender　　7. leave　　8. nuclear
9. returnee　　10. withdrawal

■問B　(a) ～ (f) にそれぞれ対応する英語表現を下記の語群から選びその番号を記せ。

(a) 不登校　　　　(b) 停学　　　　(c) 過食症
(d) 拒食症　　　　(e) 認知症　　　　(f) 養子縁組

1. adoption　　　　2. anorexia　　　　3. suspension
4. bulimia　　　　5. dementia　　　　6. truancy

■問C　(a) ～ (d) をそれぞれ英訳せよ。

(a) ネット詐欺
(b) ステマ
(c) アプリ
(d) 出会い系サイト

Chapter 8

犯罪・事件

「写真提供：iStock」

Before you read

> ➤大手回転寿司チェーンを友人と共に訪れた少年が、醤油差しの注ぎ口を舐める、未使用の湯呑を舐める、回転レーン上の寿司に指で唾液を付けるといった迷惑行為に及んだ。
> ➤友人は一連の行為を撮影し、SNS で拡散させた。同様の行為が他の回転寿司チェーンでも発生、その後、回転寿司を訪れる客が大幅に減少した。
> ➤英紙 The Guardian の 2023 年 2 月 3 日付け記事を読んでみよう。

NEWS 8

Wave of 'sushi terrorism' grips Japan's restaurant world

There are breaches of etiquette—drenching your rice in soy sauce, for one—and then there are heinous acts of "sushi terrorism". Japan's signature cuisine is at the centre of a police investigation after customers at revolving sushi restaurants posted video clips of themselves interfering with food and playing pranks on other customers.

The incidents have sent shares plummeting in a leading *kaitenzushi* and prompted operators to rethink how they serve their dishes. Several acts of what is being called "sushi terrorism" have emerged on Twitter and other social media in recent days, although some apparently date back weeks, and even years.

A clip of the most egregious culinary crime, which has been viewed almost 40m times on Twitter, shows what appears to be a teenager licking the open top of a communal soy sauce bottle and the entire rim of a teacup, which he then places back on a shelf.

If that wasn't bad enough, the 48-second clip shows him licking his finger and using it to touch two pieces of sushi, presumably ordered by another customer, as they travel past on the conveyer belt.

The video, filmed at a branch of the Sushiro chain in the central city of Gifu, prompted stocks in the restaurant's parent company to plunge nearly 5% on Tuesday. Other videos show people at other chains putting wasabi on passing pieces of sushi and licking the spoon from a container of green-tea powder that is used by multiple diners.

While the small number of incidents hardly points to a sushi crime wave, the videos have sparked uproar in Japan, where the industry is worth an estimated ¥740bn (£4.7bn/$5.7bn). Sushiro, the market leader, said this week that the man who made the viral video had apologised, along with his parents, but added that it had filed criminal and civil cases.

The clips prompted Sushiro to replace all of the restaurant's soy sauce bottles and rewash its teacups. It has also stopped placing condiments and utensils on each table at the restaurant in question and others located nearby, and is asking diners to collect them from a serving point, Japanese media reports say.

Two other chains, Hama Sushi and Kura Sushi, have also said they plan to take legal action, with the latter planning to install cameras above conveyor belts to monitor customers, Jiji press agency reported.

— Based on a report on theguardian.com on February 3, 2023 —

〈ニュース解説〉　1958 年に大阪で誕生した回転寿司は、コンベアベルトを利用することで、配膳や接客の手間を減らしコストを引き下げて「一皿 100 円」を実現し、社会に貢献してきた。また、コロナ禍に直面すると注文用のタッチパネル、機械が来店客に発行する番号札による座席案内、セルフレジなどを導入し、一層のコストダウンを実現した。今回の心なき迷惑行為が発生した背景には、入店から会計まで店員とほとんど接触しないですむまでに省力化が深化し、店員の目が行き届かなくなったという事情もある。同様の迷惑行為の再発がないことを祈るのみだ。

(Notes)　【※☞マークは *Useful Expressions*】

◆　**grip**　強い影響を与える

◆　(L. 1)　**for one**　例えば

◆　(L. 2)　**heinous**　極めて邪悪な

◆　(L. 2)　**"sushi terrorism"**　「寿司テロリズム」（日本語表現の直訳）

◆　(L. 2)　**signature cuisine**　代表的な料理

◆　(L. 3)　**after**　（ここでは because の意味に近い）

◆　(L. 3)　**revolving sushi restaurant**　回転寿司レストラン（conveyor-belt sushi restaurant などの表現も見られる）

◆　(L. 4)　**interfere with** …　（許可なく、勝手に）に手を出す

◆　(L. 4)　**play pranks on** …　（実害を与えるつもりのない）悪ふざけをする

◆　(L. 11)　**the open top of a** … **bottle**　…瓶の蓋を外した注ぎ口

◆　(L. 12)　**communal**　共用の

◆　(L. 17)　**Sushiro**　株式会社あきんどスシロー［英：Akindo Sushiro Co., Ltd.　回転寿司のチェーンを展開。本社：大阪。持株会社：（株）FOOD & LIFE COMPANIES。（株）京樽もグループ会社の 1 社。国内外で事業展開］

☞◆　(L. 23)　**an estimated ¥740bn** …　概算で 7400 億円（an estimated amount of ¥740bn の略で、例えば、「人数」の概算の場合には "an estimated number of 2000" の "number of" を省略して、"an estimated 2000" などと書かれる）

◆　(L. 25)　**viral video**　（SNS で）拡散した動画

◆　(L. 26)　**file criminal and civil cases**　刑事・民事訴訟を提起する

◆　(L. 28)　**condiment**　調味料、薬味

◆　(L. 28)　**utensils**　台所用品（ここでは、箸やスプーンなど）

☞◆　(L. 29)　**in question**　本件の、当該の

◆　(L. 31)　**Hama Sushi**　はま寿司［英：HAMA-SUSHI Co., Ltd.。本社：東京。牛丼チェーン「すき屋」を運営する（株）ゼンショーの子会社。尚、英文社名中の句点、読点に関しては各企業の書式に従うのが通例］

◆　(L. 31)　**Kura Sushi**　くら寿司（英：Kura Sushi, Inc. 本社：大阪）

☞◆　(L. 32)　**take (legal) action**　（法的な）措置を講じる

◆　(L. 33)　**Jiji press agency**　（株）時事通信社（英：Jiji Press Ltd. 本社：東京。国内に 60 か所、海外に 25 か所の支社、総支社を有する）

　　ニュースを読んで、下記の設問に答えよ。

1. 本文の内容と一致するものには T (True) を、一致しないものには F (False) を記せ。

(　　) (1) Given that sushi is Japan's signature cuisine, any breach of expected etiquette while enjoying the dish is considered an act of "sushi terrorism."

(　　) (2) The market share of a top *kaitenzushi* chain nosedived when the occurrence of "sushi terrorism" came to light.

(　　) (3) A video showed a young man drinking the contents from a shared soy sauce bottle in what appeared to be the most eccentric culinary conduct.

(　　) (4) According to the news story, a young man was presumably ordered by another customer to touch some sushi on the conveyor belt with his saliva-covered finger.

(　　) (5) The stocks in Sushiro's parent company showed a sharp negative reaction on Tuesday to the video filmed at a branch of the Sushiro chain in Gifu.

2. 本文中に揚げた［*Useful Expressions*］を参照し、下記の語群を並び替えて空欄に適語を記し、日本語に合う英文を完成させよ。

(1) その国の新型コロナウイルスによる死者数はおよそ 5 万人にのぼる。これは多くの国を大幅に下回るもので、政府によるワクチン接種の推進がその要因だ。

The country has (　　) (　　) (　　) (　　) (　　) (　　) in total—significantly lower than many other countries thanks to the government's vaccination drive.

> an　coronavirus　deaths　estimated　50,000　suffered

(2) 警察は犯罪が起きた当日の夕刻の容疑者のアリバイを確立しようとしている。

Police are trying to determine whether the suspect has an alibi (　　) (　　) (　　) (　　) (　　) (　　) (　　) (　　) when the crime was committed.

> day　evening　in　of　on　question　the（2 度使用）

(3) 万策尽きた場合には、交渉相手に対し法的措置を講じることができる。裁判は多額の費用を要するので、最後の手段とすべきである。

If all else fails, (　　) (　　) (　　) (　　) (　　) (　　) a negotiating party. Taking someone to court can be expensive so it should be (　　) (　　) (　　).

> action　against　be　can　last　legal　resort　taken　your

音声を聞き、下線部を補え。（２回録音されています。１回目はナチュラルスピード、２回目はスロースピードです。）

Natural 3 / Slow 5

　　Japanese police have arrested four men for allegedly orchestrating scams and robberies while jailed overseas, in a case that has gripped the country.

　　Authorities say they targeted the elderly, and stole or cheated their victims of billions of yen. From their jail in the Philippines, the men managed to recruit accomplices in Japan to carry out the robberies. One of them ⁽¹⁾_____ 5
_____, who calls himself "Luffy" after a popular anime character.

　　Philippine authorities deported two of them, Kiyoto Imamura and Toshiya Fujita, to Japan earlier this week. The other two—Yuki Watanabe and Tomonobu Kojima—arrived in Japan on Wednesday night. They were ⁽²⁾_____
_____ who have been arrested in the Philippines since late 2019 ⁽³⁾ 10
_____ scam crimes.

Natural 4 / Slow 6

　　Japanese authorities had been hunting down the gang ⁽⁴⁾_____
_____ in the summer of 2021. More than 50 incidents spread across 14 prefectures are said to be linked to the gang, including one which resulted in the murder of a 90-year-old woman in Tokyo in January. 15

　　The four ringleaders were already held in a Philippine jail when they began their scheme, according to reports. Using their mobile phones, they recruited for accomplices in Japan via social media, where they put up cryptic ads for "dark part-time jobs" promising lucrative pay. They would send instructions and communicate with their gang members via the encrypted app Telegram. 20

　　The accomplices would ⁽⁵⁾_____ or members of the Japan Financial Services Agency and tell victims that their accounts had been compromised, according to the Asahi Shimbun. During a subsequent visit to the victim's home, the accomplice would steal their ATM cards to withdraw all their money. 25

— *Based on a report on BBC.com on February 9, 2023* —

〈ニュース解説〉　高齢化の進行が著しい先進国では、高齢者世帯が多くの金融資産を保有している。「特殊詐欺」は、65 歳以上の面識のない不特定多数を主な標的にして、電話やメールなどを使って対面せずに現金などを搾取する。2000 年代前半から被害が拡大しており、最近では「オレオレ詐欺」、「新型コロナの還付金詐欺」、「キャッシュカード詐欺盗」、「預貯金詐欺」による被害が多い。本ニュースが報じる４人の容疑者は、フィリピンを拠点にして被害額が 60 億円にのぼる特殊詐欺グループのリーダー格とされる。特殊詐欺から強盗などに手口を凶悪化せた可能性があるとみられ、犯行グループの解明が捜査の最大の焦点となっている。

(Notes)
allegedly（真偽は別にして）申し立てによれば、伝えられるところでは　**orchestrate**（時に、密かに）支持する、組織化する　**scams and robberies**（特）詐欺と強盗　**grip** 強い影響を与える　**"Luffy"**「ルフィ」（特殊詐欺グループの指示役とされ、アニメ・ワンピースの主人公の名を模したとみられる）**Philippines authorities** フィリピン入国管理局（Republic of the Philippines Bureau of Immigration）**Kiyoto Imamura** 今村磨人　**Toshiya Fujita** 藤田聖也　**Yuki Watanabe** 渡辺優樹　**Tomonobu Kojima** 小島智信　**hunt down** 追跡して捕らえる　**gang** 犯行グループ　**spread**（自動詞の過去分詞が形容詞として使われている）　**ringleader** 主犯格、首謀者　**cryptic ad** 暗号化した広告　**"dark part-time job"**「闇バイト」（和製英語とされる）　**encrypted app Telegram** 暗号化された（メッセージ）アプリ・テレグラム　**Japan Financial Services Agency** 金融庁（日本の行政機関で金融機能の安定確保や預金者などの保護を図る）　**compromise** 傷つける、（安全システムを）破る　**Asahi Shimbun** 朝日新聞　**ATM** 現金自動預払機（automated〔automatic〕teller machine の略）

■問A　空所 (a) 〜 (k) にそれぞれ入るべき1語を下記の語群から選びその番号を記せ。

業務上過失	→	professional (a)
脱税	→	tax (b)
著作権侵害	→	copyright (c)
フィッシング詐欺	→	(d) scam
おとり捜査	→	(e) operation
捜査令状	→	search (f)
物的証拠	→	(g) evidence
状況証拠	→	(h) evidence
精神鑑定	→	(i) test
冤罪	→	(j) charge
自宅軟禁	→	house (k)

1. arrest	2. circumstantial	3. dodge	4. false
5. infringement	6. negligence	7. phishing	8. physical
9. psychiatric	10. sting	11. warrant	

■問B　(a) 〜 (q) にそれぞれ対応する英語表現を下記の語群から選びその番号を記せ。

(a) 重罪	(b) 軽犯罪	(c) 違反	(d) 名誉棄損
(e) 拘留	(f) 窃盗	(g) 万引き	(h) スパイ行為
(i) 贈収賄	(j) 監禁	(k) 襲撃	(l) 自白
(m) 大量殺人	(n) 残虐行為	(o) 銃撃	(p) 刺傷
(q) 脱走者			

1. assault	2. atrocity	3. bribery	4. confession
5. confinement	6. custody	7. defamation	8. espionage
9. felony	10. fugitive	11. massacre	12. misdemeanor
13. offense	14. shooting	15. shoplifting	16. stabbing
17. theft			

■問C　(a) 〜 (h) をそれぞれ和訳せよ。

(a) abuse	(b) charge	(c) corruption
(d) fraud	(e) interrogation	(f) ransom
(g) robbery	(h) smuggling	

裁判・法令

A State of Unconstitutionality?　違憲状態？
「写真提供：共同通信社」

Before you read

同性婚を認めないのは憲法違反かどうかで争われた全国5つの地方裁判所の裁判では、地裁によって判決が分かれている。同性どうしのカップルの結婚を認めていない民法規定は、婚姻の自由や法の下の平等を定めた憲法に違反すると主張して同性カップルの原告は違憲判決を求めたが、違憲判決よりは穏やかな違憲状態との判断が下された場合もあった。今後上級審での判決が注目される。Chapter 9 では、憲法判断を委ねられた地方裁判所がどのように対応したかに注目して読んでみよう。

NEWS 9

Fukuoka court rules same-sex marriage ban is in "state of unconstitutionality"

The Fukuoka District Court on Thursday ruled that a ban on same-sex marriage is in a "state of unconstitutionality," following a ruling last week by the Nagoya District Court with stronger phrasing clearly calling it unconstitutional. The Fukuoka court, however, rejected a demand by the plaintiffs that the government pay them each ¥1 million in damages.   5

A 35-year-old plaintiff from the city of Fukuoka said same-sex marriage is a human rights issue and strongly urged parliament to hold discussions on the matter as soon as possible. "I feel relieved that we are making progress, but I did hope that they would say it was unconstitutional," he said, referring to the stronger wording used by the Nagoya court.   10

Thursday's ruling was the fifth from among six similar lawsuits filed with courts across the country. Decisions have been split over the question of whether the ban is constitutional, with one previous ruling also using the phrase "state of unconstitutionality."

8 "Not allowing the same benefits granted to married couples, nor allowing   15
individuals the option of being family members with partners they choose, is in a state of unconstitutionality regarding Article 24, Clause 2 of the Constitution," presiding Judge Hiroyuki Ueda said in the ruling. Article 24, Clause 2 stipulates that laws be enacted from the standpoint of individual dignity and equality of the sexes with regard to choosing a spouse and marriage. But the ruling stopped short of   20
fully declaring the ban unconstitutional considering the variety of systems available, including municipalities' partnership systems, and how opinion is still divided over the issue, especially among older people.

The ruling also stated that banning same-sex marriage does not violate other articles in the Constitution, including the right to equality under Article 14. It also   25
rejected the plaintiffs' argument that the government failed to act on the issue by not drafting legislation to allow same-sex marriage. The government has said that Article 24, Clause 1 does not cover same-sex marriage because the clause says "marriage shall be based only on the mutual consent of both sexes." Thursday's ruling, along with the four previous ones, all ruled in favor of the government regarding this   30
clause.

— Based on a report on Japantimes.co.jp on June 8, 2023 —

〈ニュース解説〉　同性婚が認められないのは憲法違反かどうかを争う福岡地裁判決が出た。原告は男性カップル2組、女性カップル1組の計6人。同性婚をめぐっては2019年に全国5つの地裁（東京、大阪、札幌、名古屋、福岡）で同じような訴訟が提訴されているが、これまで4地裁の判決は、争点に関して「合憲（constitutional）」「違憲（unconstitutional）」「違憲状態（state of unconstitutionality）」と判断が分かれていた。今回5件目の地裁の判断である福岡地裁判決において原告は、憲法第24条第1項が婚姻の自由を保障していることを主張し、同2項の個人の尊厳に基づく法整備を求めている。さらに原告は、憲法第14条が法の下の平等を謳っていることを理由に、現行制度に対する違憲判断とその是正を求めた。判決では、第24条第1項の婚姻は異性間を想定しており、原告の主張は退けられた。一方、同第2項については、同性婚を認める法律が制定されていないことを重視し、個人の尊厳に基づく法制度の制定を求めた同項に違反する状態と断じ、国はこの状態を解消する立法措置に着手するように促した。一方原告は、本判決を不服として福岡高裁に控訴した。本英文記事では、全国の裁判所に提訴された6件の訴訟のうち、今回の福岡地裁判決は5番目の判決であるとしているが、これは、東京地裁では2021年3月に二次訴訟が提起されていることから、これを加えて6件と数えていると思われる。

(Notes)　【※☞マークは *Useful Expressions*】

◆ **same-sex marriage ban**　同性婚禁止（異性婚は heterosexual marriage）

◆ **state of unconstitutionality**　違憲状態（unconstitutional よりは違憲性を断定しない点で、やや弱い裁定である）

◆ (L. 1)　**The Fukuoka District Court**　福岡地方裁判所

◆ (L. 2-3)　**The Nagoya District Court**　名古屋地方裁判所

◆ (L. 4)　**plaintiff**　原告（その他に accuser や suitor が使われることもある。被告は accused や defendant）

◆ (L. 5)　**damages**　損害賠償金（damage は損害。複数で損害賠償金の意）

◆ (L. 11)　**lawsuit**　訴訟（file a lawsuit 提訴する）

◆ (L. 17)　**Article 24, Clause 2 of the Constitution**　（日本国）憲法第24条第2項

◆ (L. 18)　**presiding Judge Hiroyuki Ueda**　上田洋幸裁判長

☞◆ (L. 19)　**from the standpoint of**　～の観点（視点）から

☞◆ (L. 20)　**stop short of**　～するまでには至らない、～の寸前で止まる

◆ (L. 22)　**municipalities' partnership systems**　市（等地方公共団体）におけるパートナーシップ制度（法律上の婚姻とは相違するが、異性間の婚姻関係と違わない程度の実質を持つ性的少数者カップルに、異性婚と同等の公共サービスを提供する制度）

◆ (L. 25)　**Article 14**　（日本国憲法）第14条

◆ (L. 27-28)　**Article 24, Clause 1**　（日本国憲法）第24条第1項

◆ (L. 30)　**the four previous ones**　（福岡地裁判決）以前の4件の地裁判決（具体的には、2021年3月の札幌地裁判決、2022年6月の大阪地裁判決、2022年11月の東京地裁判決、2023年5月の名古屋地裁判決を指す。大阪地裁判決だけが、憲法第14条、第24条第1項及び第2項のすべてにおいて現行制度を合憲と判断した）

1. 本文の内容と一致するものには T (True) を、一致しないものには F (False) を記せ。

(　　) (1) The Fukuoka District Court ruling was far more radical in nature than the one issued by the district court in Nagoya on a similar case.

(　　) (2) The plaintiffs in the same-sex marriage case were fully satisfied with the decision given by the Fukuoka District Court.

(　　) (3) As the result of the rulings at the district courts nationwide, plaintiffs of the same-sex cases are extremely optimistic about their legal status in Japan.

(　　) (4) The extremely subtle difference between 'being unconstitutional' and 'being in a state of unconstitutionality' caused absolutely no problem for plaintiffs in the same-sex marriage cases.

(　　) (5) Based on the principle of the separation of powers among the three branches of government, the Fukuoka District Court decision refrained from telling the government to take a step toward legal approval of the same-sex marriage.

(　　) (6) The Japanese government maintained at the Fukuoka District Court trial that the Japanese Constitution does not refer to marriages between same-sex partners.

(　　) (7) There has been a consensus among the district court rulings on the constitutionality of the government position on the same-sex marriage ban.

(　　) (8) With regard to the same-sex marriage, Articles 14 and 24 are focal points.

2. 本文中に掲げた下記の [*Useful Expressions*] を用いて空欄に適語を記し、日本語に合う英文を完成させよ。

(1) ⟨ **from the standpoint of** ⟩

(　　　　　　　　　　　　　　　　　　　　), it is a bad decision to invest in firms in such an unstable country.

保守的なビジネス関係者の視点からすると、そのように不安定な国の企業に投資することは、誤った判断である。

(2) ⟨ **stop short of** ⟩

Many African nations (　　　　　　　　　　　　　　　　　) for its invasion in Ukraine.

多くのアフリカ諸国は、ウクライナ侵攻でロシアを非難するまでには至らなかった。

音声を聞き、下線部を補え。（２回録音されています。１回目はナチュラルスピード、２回目はスロースピードです。）

natural
9
slow
11

The federal indictment against Donald Trump and his aide Walt Nauta was unsealed Friday, providing more details about the special counsel's investigation into the former president's [^(1)] _____ .

Trump faces a total of 37 counts, including 31 counts of willful retention of national defense information, according to the indictment.   5

The former president, who has denied any wrongdoing, [^(2)] _____ _____ in a Miami courthouse on Tuesday afternoon.

natural
10
slow
12

The classified documents that Trump supposedly stored in boxes at Mar-a-Lago included information regarding defense and weapons capabilities, US nuclear programs and potential vulnerabilities of the US and its allies to a military   10 attack, the indictment said. Some were classified at the highest levels and [^(3)] _____ _____ they required special handling.

Trump [^(4)] _____ classified documents on two occasions to others, according to the indictment.

Trump told his attorney to tell the Justice Department that he didn't have the   15 documents sought by the subpoena, prosecutors say in the indictment. In addition, it alleges Trump directed Nauta to move documents to hide them from Trump's own attorneys and FBI agents and [^(5)] _____ to "hide or destroy documents" sought by the subpoena.

— Based on a report on CNN.com on June 9, 2023 —

〈ニュース解説〉　ドナルド・トランプ前大統領は、大統領退任後に連邦政府の機密文書を持ち出し、自身のフロリダ州の私邸であるマール・ア・ラーゴに私的に保管していたとして起訴された。同氏は既にニューヨーク大陪審によって別件で起訴され、米国の大統領経験者最初の起訴事例とされているが、今回の機密文書持ち出しに対する連邦大陪審による起訴で、大統領経験者が連邦法違反で起訴された最初のケースとなった。起訴状の罪状には、共謀、偽証、司法妨害、スパイ防止法違反が挙げられているが、捜査の焦点は、機密文書持ち出しが意図的なものであったのか、さらに同氏が捜査妨害をしたかの点にしぼられた。機密文書持ち出しは、バイデン大統領やペンス前副大統領も行ったが、両氏は自ら当局に連絡し即座に文書を返却、捜査にも協力している点で、トランプ氏と大きな違いを示している。

(Notes)
federal indictment 連邦法違反での起訴状［連邦大陪審（Federal Grand Jury）によって起訴］　**Walt Nauta** ウォルト・ナウタ（ホワイトハウスでトランプ前大統領の付き人として働いた後、マール・ア・ラーゴでも勤務）　**special counsel** 特別検察官（かつては special prosecutor と呼ばれた。本件では Jack Smith 氏が任命された）　**classified document** 秘密公文書　**Miami courthouse** マイアミ（連邦地方）裁判所　**Justice Department** 司法省　**subpoena** 召喚令状（文書提出令状と証人喚問令状の二つがあるがここでは前者）　**prosecutor**（上記 special counsel と同じ）特別検察官　**FBI agent** FBI 捜査官［FBI は Federal Bureau of Investigation（連邦捜査局）の略称］

■問A 空所 (a) 〜 (i) にそれぞれ入るべき 1 語を下記の語群から選びその番号を記せ。

陪審制度	→	(a) system
裁判員制度	→	(b) system
裁判長	→	(c) judge
国選弁護人	→	(d) lawyer
執行猶予付き判決	→	(e) sentence
終身刑	→	life (f)
死刑	→	death (g)
刑事訴訟	→	(h) action
民事訴訟	→	(i) action

1. civil	2. court–appointed	3. criminal	4. imprisonment
5. jury	6. lay judge	7. penalty	8. presiding
9. suspended			

■問B (a) 〜 (l) にそれぞれ対応する英語表現を下記の語群から選びその番号を記せ。

(a) 弁護士	(b) 検察官	(c) 原告
(d) 被告	(e) 裁判	(f) 起訴
(g) 証言	(h) 評決	(i) 判決
(j) 有罪判決	(k) 刑罰	(l) 恩赦

1. amnesty	2. conviction	3. defendant	4. judgment
5. lawyer	6. penalty	7. plaintiff	8. prosecution
9. prosecutor	10. testimony	11. trial	12. verdict

■問C 日本の司法制度に関係する (a) 〜 (f) の用語をそれぞれ和訳せよ。

(a) Supreme Court

(b) high court

(c) district court

(d) family court

(e) summary court

(f) Supreme Public Prosecutors Office

Chapter 10

地球環境・気象

「写真提供：iStock」

Before you read

国連の「気候変動に関する政府間パネル（IPCC＝Intergovernmental Panel on Climate Change）」は 2023 年、9 年ぶりに統合報告書を発表し、「温暖化ガスの放出をこのまま続けると短期のうちに世界の平均気温は産業革命前と比べ 1.5℃以上上昇してしまう」と警鐘を鳴らした。また、同報告書は「人間の活動が主に温暖化をもたらしたことは疑う余地がない」としたうえで、「2020 年までの 10 年間に世界の平均気温は 1.1℃上昇した」とも指摘している。Chapter 10 では温暖化ガスの排出量を算定する際、人間の活動の中でこれまで算入されることがなかった軍事部門からの排出について考える。また、自然現象であるエルニーニョが気温上昇や異常気象に及ぼす影響についても取り上げる。

NEWS 10

World's war on greenhouse gas emissions has a military blind spot

When it comes to taking stock of global emissions, there's an elephant in the room: the world's armed forces.

As temperatures hit new highs, scientists and environmental groups are stepping up pressure on the U.N. to force armies to disclose all their emissions and end a long-standing exemption that has kept some of their climate pollution off the books. 5 Among the world's biggest consumers of fuel, militaries account for 5.5% of global greenhouse gas emissions, according to a 2022 estimate by international experts.

But defence forces are not bound by international climate agreements to report or cut their carbon emissions, and the data that is published by some militaries is unreliable or incomplete at best, scientists and academics say. That's because military 10 emissions abroad, from flying jets to sailing ships to training exercises, were left out of the 1997 Kyoto Protocol on reducing greenhouse gases—and exempted again from the 2015 Paris accords—on the grounds that data about energy use by armies could undermine national security.

Now, environmental groups Tipping Point North South and The Conflict and 15 Environment Observatory, along with academics from the British universities of Lancaster, Oxford, and Queen Mary are among those pushing for more comprehensive and transparent military emissions reporting, using research papers, letter campaigns, and conferences in their lobbying drive.

In the first five months of 2023, for example, at least 17 peer reviewed papers 20 have been published, three times the number for all of 2022 and more than the previous nine years combined, according to one campaigner who tracks the research.

The groups also wrote in February to the U.N. Framework Convention on Climate Change (UNFCCC) calling on the United Nations' climate body to include all military emissions given their significance for comprehensive global carbon 25 accounting. "Our climate emergency can no longer afford to permit the 'business as usual' omission of military and conflict-related emissions within the UNFCCC process," the groups wrote.

Emissions accounting will come into focus in the first global stocktake—an assessment of how far behind countries are from the Paris climate goals—due to take 30 place at the COP28 climate summit in the United Arab Emirates starting on Nov. 30.

— *Based on a Reuters report on usnews.com on July 9, 2023* —

〈ニュース解説〉　2022 年 11 月にエジプトのシャルム・エム・シェイクで開催された国連気候変動枠組条約（下記 Notes 参照）第 27 回締約国会議（the 27th Conference of the Parties：COP27）では、パリ協定（下記 Notes 参照）に基づき地球の気温上昇を産業革命前の 1.5℃以内に抑えるという目標を実現するため、温暖化ガス排出量の削減をさらに加速させ、2030 年に 2019 年比 43 パーセント減とすることで合意した。こうした中で、世界の温暖化ガス排出量をより包括的に把握するためには、これまで国家安全保障上の理由からパリ協定の適用対象外となってきた軍事・防衛部門からの排出量も計上すべきとの声が高まってきている。同部門は世界の温暖化ガス排出全体の 6 パーセント近くを占めるとの民間による推計もあるが、はっきりしたことは分かっていないのが現状。2022 年 2 月に始まったロシアのウクライナ侵攻により両国だけではなく欧米諸国でも軍備増強が進み、それに伴い化石燃料の消費が増え、同部門からの温暖化ガスの排出がさらに増大しているのではないかとも懸念されている。

(Notes)　【※☞マークは *Useful Expressions*】

◆　**greenhouse gas**　温室効果ガス、温暖化ガス　[global warming gas も同義で、二酸化炭素（CO_2）、メタン（CH_4）、一酸化二窒素（N_2O）等、大気中の熱を吸収し地球温暖化をもたらすガスの総称。いずれの排出量も二酸化炭素換算で示される場合が多いため、"carbon" と言い換えられることもある。第 4 パラグラフ 2 行目の "carbon emission" や第 8 パラグラフ 3 行目の "global carbon emission" の carbon がその例]

◆　(L. 1)　**take stock of 〜**　〜を見積もる、評価する

◆　(L. 1)　**elephant in the room**　タブー視されていること、敢えて触れないようにしていること（原義は「部屋の中にいる象」だが、皆が気づいているにもかかわらず、触れないようにしている重大な事柄や問題を意味する）

◆　(L. 8)　**defence**　（Reuters の記事であるため英国式綴りとなっている。米国式綴りは "defense"）

☞◆　(L. 8)　**bound by 〜**　（規則、約束、慣習などに）縛られる、拘束される

◆　(L. 12)　**Kyoto Protocol**　京都議定書 [1992 年に国連環境開発会議（地球サミット）で採択された国連気候変動枠組条約（下記参照）を実施するための基本ルールとして、1997 年に京都で開催された COP3（ニュース解説参照）で採択された先進国の温暖化ガス排出削減に関する国際的な取り決め。同議定書では 2020 年までの先進国の温暖化対策の目標が示された]

◆　(L. 13)　**Paris accord**　パリ協定 [Paris agreement とも表現される。2015 年にパリで開催された COP21 で京都議定書を受け継ぐ形で 2020 年以降の温暖化防止対策について締約された協定。京都議定書と異なり、先進国だけではなく中国や途上国を含むすべての国連気候変動枠組条約締約国に対し温暖化防止対策への参加を求めている]

◆　(L. 15-16)　**Tipping Point North South and The Conflict and Environment Observatory**　ティッピング・ポイント・ノース・サウスならびにザ・コンフリクト・アンド・エンバイロメント・オブザーバトリー（いずれも国際的な環境団体）

◆　(L. 16-17)　**British Universities of Lancaster, Oxford, and Queen Mary**　ランカスター大学、オックスフォード大学、クイーンメアリー大学（いずれも英国の主要大学。Queen Mary はロンドン大学を構成するカレッジの 1 つ）

◆　(L. 20)　**peer reviewed papers**　専門家の査読を受けた論文

◆　(L. 23-24)　**U.N. Framework Convention on Climate Change**　国連気候変動枠組条約 [略称UNFCCC。1992 年に大気中の温暖化ガスを安定化させることを目標に 198 か国が参加して締約された条約。この条約に基づき、1995 年から原則 1 年に 1 度締約国会議が開催されている。この文では同条約事務局を意味する]

☞◆　(L. 25)　**given 〜**　〜を考えると、〜を前提とすると

◆　(L. 25-26)　**global carbon accounting**　世界の炭素（温暖化ガス）排出量の算定

◆　(L. 26-27)　**'business as usual'**　いつも行われていること、いつも通りのこと

◆　(L. 31)　**the United Arab Emirates**　アラブ首長国連邦（アブダビ、ドバイを中心とする 7 首長国から構成される連邦国家）

ニュースを読んで、下記の設問に答えよ。

1. 本文の内容と一致するものには T (True) を、一致しないものには F (False) を記せ。

(   ) (1) Experts estimated in 2022 that armed forces emit more than one-twentieth of global warming gas emissions.

(   ) (2) Under the Paris agreement, armed forces are allowed not to disclose their global warming gas emissions abroad.

(   ) (3) In 2022, more than 10 academic articles were published in order to campaign for clearer and more complete disclosure of military carbon emissions.

(   ) (4) Some scientists urged the UN climate body to include all greenhouse gas emissions of armed forces considering their academic importance.

(   ) (5) Assessing how countries are falling behind the goals of the Paris accord will be one of the agenda items of the COP 28 in 2023.

2. 本文に掲げた ［*Useful Expressions*］を参照し、下記の語群を並び替えて空欄に適語を記し、日本語に合う英文を完成させよ。

(1) 私は規則に縛られたくない。

I don't (   ) (   ) (   ) (   ) (   ) (   ).

be,   bound,   by,   rules,   to,   want

(2) 彼女の年齢を考えると、彼女はとても泳ぎが上手い。

(   ) (   ) (   ), (   ) (   ) a very good swimmer.

age,   given,   her,   is,   she

音声を聞き、下線部を補え。（2回録音されています。1回目はナチュラルスピード、2回目はスロースピードです。）

Natural
15

Slow
17

    Governments must prepare for more extreme weather events and record temperatures in the coming months, the World Meteorological Organization warned Tuesday, as it declared the onset of the warming phenomenon El Niño.

    El Niño is a natural climate pattern in the tropical Pacific Ocean [(1)] _____ - _____ - _____ sea-surface temperatures and has a major influence on weather across the globe, affecting billions of people.   5

    "The onset of El Niño will greatly increase the likelihood of breaking temperature records and [(2)] _____ of the world and in the ocean," said WMO Secretary-General Petteri Taalas. To save lives and livelihoods, governments must establish early warning systems and prepare for   10 further disruptive weather events this year, he said.

Natural
16

Slow
18

    The last three years have been some of the warmest on record, even with El Niño's sister phase, La Niña—which is marked by cooler-than-average ocean temperatures.

    A "double whammy" of a very strong El Niño and human-caused warming   15 from [(3)] _____ 2016 becoming the hottest year on record, according to the WMO, the United Nations' agency for weather, climate and water resources. But the first El Niño to develop in seven years layered on top of human-caused global heating, could push 2023 or 2024 to break 2016's heat record, the WMO said.   20

    Along with increased ocean warming, El Niño events are [(4)] _____ _____ southern South America, the southern United States, the Horn of Africa and central Asia. But it can also amplify [(5)] _____ _____ Australia, Indonesia, parts of southern Asia, Central America, and northern South America. Other impacts include dangerous tropical cyclones in the   25 Pacific and the mass bleaching of fragile coral reefs.

— Based on a report on CNN.com on July 5, 2023 —

〈ニュース解説〉　エルニーニョ現象とは、太平洋赤道周辺海域で海面水温が平年より高くなり、その状態が1年以上続く現象。一方、ラニーニャは同海域の海面水温が平年より低い状態が続く現象。それぞれ数年おきに発生する。エルニーニョは世界の多くの地域に猛暑や様々な異常気象を引き起こす可能性が高い。2023年7月、世界気象機関は7年ぶりにエルニーニョが発生したと宣言し、各国政府に対して健康、生態系、経済への影響を抑えるための準備を呼びかけた。今回のエルニーニョは2029年までに世界経済に約3兆ドル（約433兆円）の損失をもたらすと予想する向きもある。日本ではエルニーニョが発生すると冷夏や長雨などの天候不順に陥ることが多かったが、人間の活動がもたらした地球温暖化と2023年初めまで続いたラニーニャの影響が相まって、日本でも2023年は高温傾向が続くと予想されている。

(Notes)
World Meteorological Organization 世界気象機関（国連の専門機関の一つで、世界の気象業務の調和と統一のとれた業務推進に必要な企画・調整活動にあたっている。略称 WMO。本部はジュネーブ）　**El Niño** エルニーニョ（ニュース解説を参照。原義はスペイン語で「男の子」）　**WMO Secretary-General Petteri Taalas** ペッテリ・ターラス WMO 事務局長　**La Niña** ラニーニャ（ニュース解説参照。原義はスペイン語で「女の子」であるため、ここでは "El Niño's sister phase" と表現されている）　**double whammy** ダブルパンチ　**Horn of Africa** アフリカの角（インド洋と紅海に向かって角のように突き出たアフリカ大陸東部の呼称。エチオピア、ソマリア、ケニア、ジブチ、エリトリアがこの地域に含まれる。2020年10月から雨不足に見舞われ、すでに過去40年で最悪の干ばつ被害が出ている）　**mass bleaching of fragile coral reefs** 脆弱なサンゴ礁の大規模な白化現象（サンゴの赤色は褐虫藻というプランクトンによるもの。褐虫藻はサンゴと共生し栄養をもたらしているが、水温が高くなるとサンゴから抜けていなくなってしまう。その結果、サンゴは白くなり、栄養がとれなくなるため死滅してしまう）

■問A　空所 (a) 〜 (g) にそれぞれ入るべき 1 語を下記の語群から選びその番号を記せ。

光化学スモッグ　　　→　(a) smog

生物多様性　　　　　→　biological (b)

排ガス規制　　　　　→　(c) control

放射性廃棄物　　　　→　(d) waste

絶滅危惧種　　　　　→　(e) species

永久凍土の溶解　　　→　(f) thawing

産業革命前の気温　　→　(g) temperatures

> 1. diversity,　　　2. emission,　　　3. endangered,　　4. permafrost,
> 5. photochemical,　6. pre-industrial,　7. radioactive

■問B　(a) 〜 (r) をそれぞれ和訳せよ。

(a) ecosystem

(b) ozone layer depletion

(c) environmentalist

(d) environmentally friendly

(e) pollutant

(f) deforestation

(g) desertification

(h) greenhouse gases

(i) extreme weather

(j) cold wave

(k) Japan Meteorological Agency

(l) flood warning

(m) rescuers

(n) drought

(o) evacuation center

(p) volcanic eruption

(q) aftershock

(r) tidal wave

Chapter 11

エネルギー・資源

「写真提供：iStock」

Before you read

日本政府は 2030 年度までに温室効果ガスの排出を 2013 年度比で 46 パーセント削減すること、また、2050 年までにはカーボンニュートラル（温暖化ガス排出実質ゼロ）を実現することを国際社会に公約している。その実現に向けて、化石燃料から太陽光や地熱などの再生可能エネルギーや水素・アンモニアなどの新エネルギーへの転換、ガソリン車から電気自動車への転換等、様々な取り組みが現在官民をあげて推進されている。Chapter 11 では、水素エネルギーと電気自動車搭載用蓄電を扱った記事を中心に、脱炭素社会に向けた動きについて考える。

NEWS 11

Japan aims to boost hydrogen supply to 12 million T by 2040

(19)   Japan is to revise its hydrogen strategy by the end of May with an ambitious target to boost annual supply to 12 million tonnes by 2040, the industry ministry said on Tuesday, as competition increases in the global market for the fuel.

Japanese Prime Minister Fumio Kishida on Tuesday addressed a ministerial meeting on the need to revise the hydrogen strategy, which was first mapped out in 5 2017, and accelerate the development of supply chains.

Citing massive hydrogen investment by the United States and Europe, Kishida said Japan will speed up the roll out of supply chains in cooperation with Australia, the Middle East, and Asia.

(20)   The resource poor country will also advance the development of domestic 10 regulation and support, Kishida said.

The industry ministry aims to complete the new plans in about two months' time, including for investment of 15 trillion yen ($113 billion) over 15 years in the public and private sectors, as it aims to lead the setting of global standards for the cleaner fuel, an official at the ministry told reporters. 15

Japan's existing goal is to increase annual hydrogen supply to about 3 million tonnes in 2030 from 2 million tonnes now, which is mainly used by oil refiners, and to expand the figure to 20 million tonnes in 2050, according to the ministry.

Hydrogen has been touted as a clean alternative to fossil fuels, and major industries, including energy, steel and chemicals, are looking at how to switch to 20 hydrogen to reduce carbon emissions. Its carbon footprint depends on the energy source used to produce it. The fuel, together with ammonia, has a major role in helping Japan to meet its target of becoming carbon neutral by 2050.

— Based on a report on Reuters.com on April 4, 2023 —

〈ニュース解説〉　水素は水から作ることができ、燃焼しても温暖化ガスや硫黄酸化物を排出しないため、環境への負荷が少ないクリーンな次世代エネルギーとして注目を集めている。水素は宇宙に最も多く存在する元素でもあり、天然資源を利用する再生可能エネルギーよりも安定供給が可能で、化石燃料の乏しい国でもエネルギー自給率を高めることができる。また、エネルギー効率が高く、貯蔵することができ災害時のエネルギー源として使用可能などのメリットもある。日本政府は水素を燃料とする燃料電池車（FCV：Fuel Cell Vehicle）や水素エネルギーを使った発電などの普及を目指して 2017 年に「水素基本戦略」を策定した。しかし、欧米諸国もこうした分野の技術開発や投資に熱心で国際競争がさらに高まってきていることを鑑み、2023 年にこの戦略を改定し、水素エネルギーの普及に向けて今後 15 年間に官民で 15 兆円を超える投資を行い、さらに 2040 年には水素供給量を現在の 6 倍の 1200 万トンまで増大する方針を打ち出している。ただし、水素社会の実現に向けては、「水素は石油などの化石燃料と比べて製造コストが高く需要がなかなか伸びない」、「水素ステーションなどのコストがかさむためインフラ整備がなかなか進まない」、「爆発の危険性がある」等の課題もある。

(Notes) 【※☞マークは *Useful Expressions*】

◆ **hydrogen strategy**　水素戦略（ここでは日本政府の「水素基本戦略」を指す。basic hydrogen plan と表現される場合もある）

◆ **12 million tonnes**　1200 万メートル・トン［tonne=metric ton（1000 キログラム）、メートル・トンは重量の国際標準単位。トンにはその他に short ton（907.185 キログラム）や long ton（1016.047 キログラム）もあるが、tonne と綴られている場合には通常は metric ton を意味する］

◆ (L. 2)　**the industry ministry**　経済産業省（正式名称は the Ministry of Economy, Trade and Industry）

◆ (L. 4)　**ministerial meeting**　閣僚会議（ここでは「再生可能エネルギー・水素等関係閣僚会議」を指す）

☞◆ (L. 5)　**map out ～**　～の計画を（綿密に）立てる、打ち出す

◆ (L. 8)　**roll out**　導入、稼働、展開（rollout とも綴る）

◆ (L. 10)　**the resource-poor country**　（資源の乏しい国、すなわち Japan を言い換えた表現）

◆ (L. 12)　**in about two months' time**　約 2 か月で（英国式の表現。in about two months と同義）

◆ (L. 14)　**the cleaner fuel**　（よりクリーンな燃料、すなわち hydrogen を言い換えた表現）

☞◆ (L. 19)　**be touted as ～**　～とうたわれる、～ともてはやされる、～と売り込まれる

◆ (L. 21)　**carbon footprint**　カーボン・フットプリント［商品やサービスのライフサイクル全般（原材料調達から廃棄・リサイクルまで）で排出される温暖化ガスの量を、二酸化炭素に換算した数値。CFP と略す］

◆ (L. 21)　**the energy source used to produce it**　水素の生成に用いられるエネルギー源（太陽光や風力などの再生可能エネルギー由来の電力が使われれば生成過程で二酸化炭素を排出しない「グリーン水素」が得られるが、石炭や天然ガス由来の電力を使った場合には二酸化炭素が排出されることになる）

◆ (L. 22)　**ammonia**　アンモニア（水素と同様に燃焼時に二酸化炭素を出さない新エネルギーとして注目されている）

1. 本文の内容と一致するものには T (True) を、一致しないものには F (False) を記せ。

　　(　　　) (1) The Japanese government will set a goal of increasing annual hydrogen supply sixfold by 2040.

　　(　　　) (2) The basic hydrogen strategy was initially formulated more than a decade ago by the Japanese government.

　　(　　　) (3) There is fierce international competition in the field of hydrogen supply.

　　(　　　) (4) Prime Minister Kishida said Japan would cooperate more closely with the US and Europe to accelerate the development of supply chains.

　　(　　　) (5) Ammonia is considered to be a more effective alternative to fossil fuels than hydrogen to cut carbon emissions.

2. 本文に掲げた［*Useful Expressions*］を参照し、下記の語群を並び替えて空欄に適語を記し、日本語に合う英文を完成させよ。

　(1) 行動を起こす前に戦略的な計画を綿密に立てる必要がある。

　　You need (　　　　) (　　　　) (　　　　) (　　　　) (　　　　)
　　(　　　) (　　　) (　　　　) act.

　　> a,　before,　map,　out,　plan,　strategic,　to,　you

　(2) 日本のサブカルチャーのメッカとうたわれてきたその町はいつも外国人客で一杯だ。

　　The town, which (　　　　) (　　　　) (　　　　) (　　　　) (　　　　)
　　(　　　) (　　　　) (　　　　) (　　　　), (　　　　) (　　　　) full
　　of foreign visitors.

　　> always,　as,　been,　for,　has,　is,　Japanese,　mecca,
　　> subculture,　the,　touted

音声を聞き、下線部を補え。（２回録音されています。１回目はナチュラルスピード、２回目はスロースピードです。）

Natural
21
Slow
23

Japan's industry ministry said Friday it will provide up to 117.8 billion yen ($840 million) in subsidies to Toyota Motor Corp. for its development of cutting-edge electric vehicle batteries within the country.

The move comes as the government is ⁽¹⁾ _____ domestic development of key technologies such as batteries and semiconductors. The government support is part of 127.6 billion yen ⁽²⁾ _____ seven projects to develop and invest in battery parts and materials, also including those by battery manufacturers, the ministry said. 5

It follows a decision in April to provide a subsidy of around 160 billion yen for an EV battery manufacturing project by Honda Motor Co. and GS Yuasa Corp. 10

Natural
22
Slow
24

"I hope large-scale investments by Toyota and others will significantly strengthen our country's battery supply chain" ⁽³⁾ _____ batteries, Economy, Trade and Industry Minister Yasutoshi Nishimura said at a press conference.

The government earmarked 331.6 billion yen ⁽⁴⁾ _____ support for investment and development of batteries as well as battery parts and materials. Toyota plans to expand its ⁽⁵⁾ _____ and sell 1.5 million EVs annually by 2026. 15

Also on Friday, the ministry announced it will provide up to 55 billion yen in subsidies for eight projects involving semiconductors and related parts and materials. 20

— *Based on a Kyodo News report on June 16, 2023* —

〈ニュース解説〉　世界が脱炭素社会の実現を目指す中、電気自動車（EV＝electric vehicle）の生産拡大が急速に進んできており、EV搭載用リチウムイオン蓄電池の安定供給が経済安全保障上も急務となっている。主原料であるリチウムは希少資源であり、産出はオーストラリア、チリ、中国、アルゼンチンの４か国に集中しているため、国際情勢等に伴い供給が不安定化するリスクもある。日本政府は電気自動車のさらなる普及を後押しするため、日本国内でのリチウムイオン蓄電池の開発や増産を推進すべく、自動車メーカー等に補助金を出すなどの支援を行うと共に、この分野への大規模な投資を民間部門にも促している。なお、トヨタ自動車は現在使われている電解質が液体のリチウムイオン電池よりもさらに性能面ですぐれた電解質が固体の全固体電池に転換していく、水素を燃料とする燃料電池車（FCV）を強化していくなど、多角的な方法で脱炭素化に取り組む方針を表明している。

(Notes)
Toyota Motor Corp. トヨタ自動車株式会社　**Honda Motor Co.** 本田技研工業株式会社　**GS Yuasa Corp.** 株式会社ジーエス・ユアサ・コーポレーション（自動車用・産業用電池や電源システムを製造・販売する日本企業）　**Economy, Trade and Industry Minister Yasutoshi Nishimura** 西村康稔経済産業大臣　**earmark**（資金、予算などを）確保する、割り当てる、計上する［原義は「羊の耳に所有者の印をつける」あるいはそうした印のこと］

■問A (a) 〜 (n) をそれぞれ和訳せよ。

(a) solar cell

(b) renewable energy

(c) geothermal power production

(d) wave-energy power station

(e) hydroelectric power plant

(f) nuclear power generation

(g) thermal power generation

(h) biofuel

(i) fossil fuel

(j) energy conservation

(k) power grid

(l) power shortage

(m) blackout

(n) liquified natural gas

■問B (a) 〜 (e) をそれぞれ和訳せよ。

(a) urban mine

(b) nonferrous metals

(c) proven oil reserves

(d) food security

(e) food waste

Chapter 12

人口問題

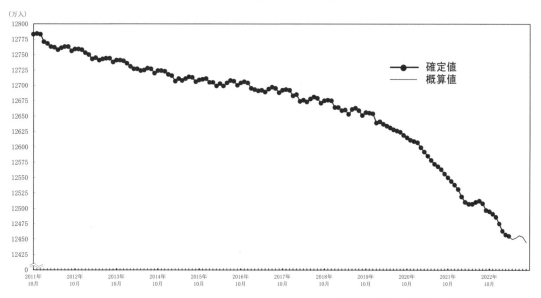

日本の総人口の推移

出典：「人口推計」（総務省統計局）

Before you read

世界人口はその増加速度が鈍化してはいるものの、平均寿命の伸びや死亡率の低下などを反映して増加し続けている。国連によると、2022年にはすでに80億人を超えており、2080年代にピークの104億人に達し、その後減少する見込みである。今後2050年までに予想される世界の人口増の半分はアフリカのサハラ以南の国々におけるものである。一方、世界の61か国・地域では2050年までにそれぞれの人口の1パーセント以上が減少するものと予想されている。急速に少子化が進む日本に関しては、国立社会保障・人口問題研究所によると、2070年の総人口が現在の70パーセントに当たる8700万人程度に減少する見込みである。Chapter 12では日本ならびに世界の人口問題について考える。

NEWS 12

Japan's population drops by half a million in 2022

Disk 2

25

Japan's population has fallen for the 12th consecutive year, as deaths rise and the birth rate continues to sink, according to government data released Wednesday.

The population stood at 124.49 million in 2022, representing a decline of 556,000 from the previous year, figures show. That figure represents both the natural change in population—meaning deaths and births—and the flow of people entering ⁵ and exiting the country.

"It is essential to take firm measures to address the declining birthrate, which is a major factor in the decline in population, as one of the top priority issues to be addressed," said Chief Cabinet Secretary Hirokazu Matsuno in a news conference on Wednesday. ¹⁰

Japan has one of the lowest birth rates in the world, as well as one of the highest life expectancies. In 2020, nearly one in 1,500 people in Japan was age 100 or older, according to government data.

That means a swelling elderly population, shrinking workforce, and not enough young people to fill in the gaps, posing a demographic crisis decades in the making. ¹⁵

26

The situation is so dire that Japan's Prime Minister Fumio Kishida warned lawmakers in January that the country is "on the brink of not being able to maintain social functions" due to the falling birth rate. He added that child-rearing support was the government's "most important policy," and solving the issue "simply cannot wait any longer." ²⁰

In April, Japan launched its new Children and Families Agency, which focuses on measures to support parents such as establishing more daycare centers and provides youth services such as counseling.

Previous similar initiatives, often carried out by local authorities, have so far failed to turn things around. Busy urban lifestyles and long working hours leave little ²⁵ time for some Japanese to start families, and the rising costs of living mean having a baby is simply too expensive for many young people.

In 2022, Japan was ranked one of the world's most expensive places to raise a child, according to research from financial institution Jefferies. And yet, the country's economy has stalled since the early 1990s, meaning frustratingly low wages and little ³⁰ upward mobility.

— Based on a report on CNN.com on April 13, 2023 —

〈ニュース解説〉 2022年に日本国内で生まれた子供（外国籍を含む）の数は1899年の統計開始以来初めて80万人を下回った。また、同年の日本の合計特殊出生率（下記Notesを参照）も過去最低レベルまで低下した。こうした急速な少子化に歯止めをかけようと政府は「こども未来戦略方針」を打ち出し、2024年から3年間に年間3兆5千万円を投じ、子供のいる家庭への支援を強化し、「異次元の少子化対策」を図ろうとしている。

(Notes) 【※☞マークは *Useful Expressions*】

◆ (L. 2)　**government data released Wednesday**　（2023年4月12日に総務省が発表した2022年10月1日現在の人口推計を指す）

◆ (L. 4-6)　**the natural change in population—meaning deaths and births—and the flow of people entering and exiting the country**　人口の自然増減（出生数と死亡数の差）ならびに流入者数と流出者数の差 ［一国の人口増減は出生数と死亡数を比べた自然増減と流入人口と流出人口を比べた社会増減により算定される］

◆ (L. 7)　**birthrate**　出生率［ここでは、"total fertility rate"（合計特殊出生率）を指す。この数値は15〜49歳の女性が一生のうちに生む子供の数の平均値を示すもので、2023年6月2日に厚生省が発表した2022年の日本の合計特殊出生率は1.26と過去最低の2005年と並ぶ数値まで下落した。UNFPA（世界人口基金、Exercise 2 Notes参照）が2023年に発表した合計特殊出生率の世界平均は2.3。世界首位がニジェールの6.7で、チャド、コンゴ共和国、ソマリアなどアフリカ諸国が上位を占めている。韓国や香港ではすでに1を切っており、韓国政府が2023年に発表した同国の2022年の合計特殊出生率は0.78で、OECD（経済協力開発機構）加盟諸国中最低となっている］

◆ (L. 9)　**Chief Cabinet Secretary Hirokazu Matsuno**　松野博一官房長官

◆ (L. 12)　**life expectancy**　平均寿命［average life expectancyとも言う。WHO（世界保健機関）が2023年に発表したデータでは、平均寿命が世界で最も長いのは日本で84.3歳。最下位はアフリカ南部のレソトで、50.7歳。世界全体の平均寿命は73.3歳。男女別では日本の女性の平均寿命は86.9歳で世界最長だが、日本の男性については、81.5歳でスイスにつぎ世界第2位だった］

◆ (L. 14)　**workforce**　労働力人口（15歳以上で、働く意思と能力の持つ人の数。就業者と完全失業者の合計）

◆ (L. 15)　**decades in the making**　今後数十年にわたり（"in the making"は「進行中」の意味）

☞◆ (L. 17)　**on the brink of 〜**　（破滅、危機など良くないこと）の瀬戸際にある、に瀕している

◆ (L. 21)　**Children and Families Agency**　こども家庭庁（「こども政策の新たな推進体制に関する基本方針」に基づき「こどもがまんなか社会」の実現に向け2023年4月に発足。総理大臣直属の内閣府外局で、従来内閣府や厚生労働省などが担ってきたこども及びこどものある家庭の福祉や健康の増進を支援するための事務が一元化された）

◆ (L. 24)　**initiatives**　問題解決のための取り組み、構想、戦略

☞◆ (L. 25)　**turn things around**　事態をがらりと変える、好転させる（"turn around 〜 "は「〜の向きを変える」）

◆ (L. 29)　**Jefferies**　ジェフリーズ（米国のJefferies Financial Groupのこと。世界有数の金融機関で、投資銀行ビジネスや資産管理、調査などの業務を行っている）

ニュースを読んで、下記の設問に答えよ。

1. 本文の内容と一致するものには T (True) を、一致しないものには F (False) を記せ。

(   ) (1) The only reason for the decrease in the Japanese population is the falling birthrate.

(   ) (2) Prime Minister Kishida said that Japan should implement measures to support child-rearing immediately.

(   ) (3) Some Japanese young people are not wealthy enough to raise a family.

(   ) (4) The Japanese government established a new government agency just for providing financial support for parents.

(   ) (5) According to a survey by Jefferies, it is less expensive to raise a child in most other countries than in Japan.

2. 本文中に掲げた［*Useful Expressions*］を参照し、下記の語群を並び替えて空欄に適語を記し、日本語に合う英文を完成させよ。

(1) 世界経済の減速を受けて、その国は債務不履行に陥る瀬戸際に瀕している。

The country (   ) (   ) (   ) (   ) (   )
(   ) (   ) the global economic slowdown.

> brink,   default,   following,   is,   of,   on,   the

(2) わが社は半年前には倒産しそうだったが、新しい CEO（最高経営責任者）がコスト削減を行い、巻き返しに成功した。

Our company was almost bankrupt six months ago, but the new CEO
(   ) (   ) (   ) (   ) (   ) (   )
(   ) (   ).

> around,   by,   costs,   cutting,   in,   succeeded,   things,   turning

音声を聞き、下線部を補え。（２回録音されています。１回目はナチュラルスピード、２回目はスロースピードです。）

Natural
(27)
Slow
(29)

India has overtaken China as the world's most populous country, according to UN population estimates, ⁽¹⁾ _____ since records began.

According to the UN's projections, which are calculated through a variety of factors including census data and birth and death rates, India now has a population of 1,425,775,850, surpassing China for the first time.   5

It is also the first time since 1950, when the UN first began keeping global population records, that ⁽²⁾ _____ .

Natural
(28)
Slow
(30)

China's population decline follows decades of strict laws to ⁽³⁾ _____, including the introduction of a one-child policy in   10
the 1980s. This included fines for having extra children, and forced abortions and sterilisations.

Recent policies introduced in China trying to ⁽⁴⁾ _____ have done little to stimulate population growth. Women still have only 1.2 children and the population is expected to fall by almost 10% in the next   15
two decades. According to projections, the size of the Chinese population could drop below 1 billion before the end of the century.

In India, the population has grown by more than a billion since 1950. Though growth has now slowed, the number of people in the country is still expected to continue to rise for the next few decades, ⁽⁵⁾ _____   20
_____. Today on average 86,000 babies are born a day in India compared with just 49,400 in China.

— Based on a report on theguardian.com on April 23, 2023 —

〈ニュース解説〉 2023 年 4 月に国連人口基金（UNFPA：United Nations Population Fund）は、2023 年にインドが中国を抜いて世界で最も人口が多い国になる見込みであると発表した。中国は長年にわたり世界人口首位の座を占めていたが、近年少子高齢化が進み、2016 年にはこれを食い止めるため「一人っ子」政策を廃止した。さらに 2021 年には第三子の出産を認める政策に転じたが、出生率の急速な低下に歯止めがかからず、2022 年に初めて死亡率が出生率を上回り、人口は減少に転じた。インドでも出生率は低下してきているものの、乳児死亡率が下がってきていることなどを背景に人口増加が続いている。

(Notes)

UN population estimates [国連人口基金（United Nations Population Fund：略称 UNFPA）が発表した世界人口推計を指す。旧称の国連人口活動基金（United Nations Fund for Population Activities）の略称を現在も使用している。同基金は国際的な資金によって開発途上国や経済移行国に人口関連の支援を行う機関で、本部をニューヨークに置く] **census data** 国勢調査のデータ（インドでは 10 年に一度の国勢調査が 2021 年に予定されていたが、コロナウイルス流行の影響で 2024 年まで延期された。そのため、2022 年の世界人口推計にインドの最新データは反映されていない） **one-child policy** 一人っ子政策（人口増による食料不足を懸念した中国共産党が 1980 年頃導入した人口抑制政策。この政策により同国の人口は 2007 年の 2500 万人から 2007 年には 1600 万人に減少したが、その結果、急速に少子高齢化が進むこととなった） **sterilisation** 不妊手術（この語には「殺菌」、「滅菌」などの意味もある。英国メディア *The Guardian* で報じられた記事なので、英国式綴り "sterilisation" となっている。米国式綴りは "sterilization"）

■問A　空所 (a) 〜 (i) にそれぞれ入るべき 1 語を下記の語群から選びその番号を記せ。

合計特殊出生率	→	total (a) rate
死亡率	→	(b) rate
人口密度が高い地域	→	(c) populated area
人口密度が低い地域	→	(d) populated area
人口過密地域	→	(e) area
過疎化地域	→	(f) area
人口動向	→	(g) trend
少子高齢化	→	(h) birthrate and (i) population

> 1. aging　2. declining　3. demographic　4. densely　5. depopulated
> 6. fertility　7. mortality　8. overpopulated　9. sparsely

■問B　(a) 〜 (l) をそれぞれ和訳せよ。

(a) equal employment opportunity

(b) emerging countries

(c) least developed countries

(d) income gap

(e) minimum wage

(f) health insurance

(g) nursing home

(h) gerontology

(i) working age population

(j) dependent

(k) spouse

(l) parental leave

Chapter 13

科学・技術

（A）太陽の核融合

「写真提供：iStock」

（B）米ローレンス・リバモア国立研究所で行われていた実験

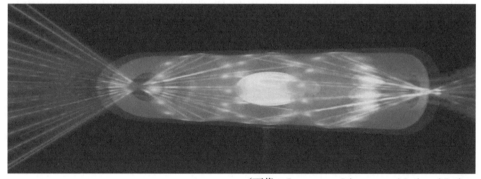

（画像：Lawrence Livermore National Laboratory）

Before you read

➤太陽内部で起きている核融合反応を人工的に地球上で再現する取り組みで、科学者にとっての長年の悲願となっている。

➤上図は米エネルギー省傘下の研究所が 2022 年末に行った実験のイラスト。長さ約 10 ミリ、直径約 5 ミリの合金製シリンダー内に冷凍した重水素と三重水素を混合した直径約 2 ミリの小球が挿入されている。

➤太陽のような高温・高圧を実験室規模で模倣し核融合を引き起こすために、シリンダーの両端にある穴から小球を標的に 192 本のレーザー光が一斉に発射されている。

➤将来、地球に商業規模の「ミニ太陽」を作ることができるのか、News 13 で読んでみよう。

NEWS 13

Nuclear fusion breakthrough a milestone for the future of clean energy, US officials say

Disk 2

(31) CNN—US Department of Energy officials announced a history-making accomplishment in nuclear fusion Tuesday: For the first time in the world, US scientists produced more energy from fusion than the laser energy they used to power the experiment.

A so-called "net energy gain" is a major milestone in a decades-long attempt 5 to source clean, limitless energy from nuclear fusion, the reaction that happens when two or more atoms are fused together. The experiment put in 2.05 megajoules of energy to the target and resulted in 3.15 megajoules of fusion energy output, generating more than 50% more energy than was put in. It's the first time an experiment resulted in a meaningful gain of energy. 10

The breakthrough was made by a team of scientists at the Lawrence Livermore National Laboratory's National Ignition Facility in California on December 5, a facility the size of a sports stadium and equipped with 192 lasers.

(32) Energy Secretary Jennifer Granholm on Tuesday called the breakthrough a "milestone." "Ignition allows us to replicate, for the first time, certain conditions 15 that are only found in the stars and sun," Granholm said. "This milestone moves us one significant step closer to the possibility of zero-carbon, abundant fusion energy powering our society."

"This is what it looks like for America to lead, and we're just getting started," Granholm also said, adding, "If we can advance fusion energy, we could use it to 20 produce clean electricity to power all segments of our economy." Arati Prabhakar, director of the White House Office of Science and Technology Policy noted, "It's a century since we figured out it was fusion that was going on in our sun and all the other stars. In that century it took so many different kinds of advances that ultimately came together to the point that we could replicate that fusion activity in a laboratory." 25

We are still a very long way from having nuclear fusion power the electric grid, experts caution. The US project, while groundbreaking, only produced enough energy to boil about 2.5 gallons of water, Tony Roulstone, a fusion expert from the engineering department at the University of Cambridge, told CNN.

That may not seem like much, but the experiment is still hugely significant 30 because scientists demonstrated that they can create more energy than they started with. While there are many more steps until this can be commercially viable, that is a major hurdle to cross with nuclear fusion, experts say.

— Based on a report on CNN.com on December 13, 2022 —

〈ニュース解説〉「核融合」は化石燃料の枯渇懸念から 1960 年代に本格的な研究が始まった。二酸化炭素を発生しないので、地球温暖化対策の切り札となる可能性も秘める。核融合は太陽と同じ核融合反応を地球上で再現する試みであり、「地上の太陽」とも呼ばれる。核融合の燃料として使われる「原子核」にはいくつかの選択肢があるが、本ニュースが取り上げている「米ローレンス・リバモア国立研究所」の敷地内に位置する「国立点火施設」（National Ignition Facility）では「重水素」と「トリウム（三重水素）」を融合させて「ヘリウム」に変え、その過程で発生するエネルギーを発電に利用する方法が研究されている。理論上は 1 グラムの燃料から石油 8 トン分のエネルギーが発生する。重水素は海水中に豊富に含まれ、三重水素は核融合炉の中で中性子を使って作られる。燃料の供給を止めれば反応が止まるため、従来の原発と比べ、安全性が高いとされる。現在、「地上の太陽」の実現を目指す複数のプロジェクトが世界で進行中だが、商用規模を可能にする技術が完成するまでには数十年を要すると言われている。

(Notes)

◆ **nuclear fusion**　核融合（「核分裂」は nuclear fission）

◆ **breakthrough**　突破口、ブレークスルー

◆ (L. 1)　**US Department of Energy**　米エネルギー省

◆ (L. 3)　**laser energy**　レーザー光のエネルギー

◆ (L. 3)　**power the experiment**　（核融合の）実験にエネルギーを供給する（supply energy to carry out nuclear fusion といった意味）

◆ (L. 5)　**net energy gain**　エネルギーの純増

◆ (L. 7)　**megajoule**　メガジュール（100 万ジュール。仕事・エネルギー・熱量の単位。1 メガジュールは 238.889 キロカロリー）

◆ (L. 8)　**target**　標的、ターゲット（*Before you read* の（B）ポイント 3 を参照）

◆ (L. 11)　**Lawrence Livermore National Laboratory**　ローレンス・リバモア国立研究所（カリフォルニア州にある米エネルギー省が所有する研究所。1952 年に核兵器の研究開発を目的に設立され、物理学、エネルギー、環境、バイオテクノロジーなどの研究を行っている）

◆ (L. 12)　**National Ignition Facility**　国立点火施設〔略称：NIF。ローレンス・リバモア国立研究所の敷地内に位置する〕

◆ (L. 14)　**Energy Secretary Jennifer Granholm**　米エネルギー省長官ジェニファー・グランホルム

◆ (L. 15)　**ignition**　点火（"ignition" は核融合関連で用いられる場合、「核融合反応が、自らが産出するエネルギーで持続し、産出エネルギー量が反応を引き起こすために用いられた投入エネルギー量を上回る状態」を意味する）

◆ (L. 15)　**certain conditions**　（ここでは、太陽などの恒星の核融合反応を可能とする超高温・高圧の環境を指す）

◆ (L. 19)　**get started**　開始する

◆ (L. 21)　**Arati Prabhakar, director of the White House Office of Science and Technology Policy**　アラティ・プラバカー大統領府科学技術政策局長官（米国内外の科学技術の動向に関して大統領に助言・勧告することを任務とする）

☞◆ (L. 26)　**still a long way from …**　…には未だほど遠い

◆ (L. 26)　**having nuclear fusion power the electric grid**　（have が使役動詞で power が the electric grid を目的語とする動詞であることに注意）

◆ (L. 26)　**electric grid**　送電網

◆ (L. 28)　**Tony Roulstone**　トニー・ルールストン（英国ケンブリッジ大学のエンジニアリング学部の原子力エネルギーを研究）

☞◆ (L. 30)　**may not seem like much**　大したものではないように思えるかもしれない

☞◆ (L. 33)　**a major hurdle to cross**　乗り越えなければならない大きな障害

ニュースを読んで、下記の設問に答えよ。

1. 本文の内容と一致するものには T (True) を、一致しないものには F (False) を記せ。

(   ) (1) In a groundbreaking achievement, US scientists triggered nuclear fusion in their lab, consuming more energy than it produced.

(   ) (2) Net energy gain in nuclear fusion is defined as a phenomenon where energy output exceeds energy input at least by 50%.

(   ) (3) The ignition facility is built on the site of a former sports stadium because a system capable of accurately irradiating 192 laser beams to a target requires a huge space.

(   ) (4) Without the achievement of net energy gain, the prospect of a society being served by abundant fusion energy with zero carbon emissions would not be possible.

(   ) (5) The US Energy Secretary believes that the United States is now capable of taking a leadership role in advancing nuclear fusion technology on a global scale.

2. 本文中に揚げた ［*Useful Expressions*］ を参照し、下記の語群を並び替えて空欄に適語を記し、日本語に合う英文を完成させよ。

(1) プロジェクトは完成から未だほど遠い。コストを抑えながら、出来る限り早期の完成に向けてスピードアップを図らねばならない。

The project is still (   ) (   ) (   ) (   ) (   ). We must step up our efforts for the earliest possible completion while keeping the cost down.

a	completion	from	long	way

(2) その企業の今年度の売上高は対前年比で 10 % 上昇する見込み。大した上昇率とは思えないかも知れないが、中国市場の景気減速を考慮にいれれば、高い評価に値する。

The company's sales for the current fiscal year are expected to rise by 10%. This may not (   ) (   ) (   ) (   ) (   ) (   ), but considering the slowdown in the Chinese market, that would deserve high recognition.

an	improvement	like	much	of	seem

(3) その企業は借入金の銀行への返済にかんして今大きな障害に直面している。どのようにこの難題に対処するかが会社の将来に影響する。

The firm is currently encountering a (   ) (   ) (   ) (   ) (   ) the repayment of its debts to banks. How it will tackle the challenge will impact its future.

concerning	cross	hurdle	significant	to

Natural
33
Slow
35

Accountants are among the professionals whose careers are most exposed to the capabilities of generative artificial intelligence, according to a new study. The researchers found that at least half of accounting tasks could be
(1) _____.

The same was true for mathematicians, interpreters, writers, and nearly 20% of the U.S. workforce, according to the study by researchers at the University of Pennsylvania and OpenAI, the company that makes the popular AI tool ChatGPT.   5

The tool has provoked excitement and anxiety in companies, schools, governments and the general public for its ability to process massive amounts of information and generate sophisticated—(2) _____ —   10
content in response to prompts from users.

Natural
34
Slow
36

The researchers, who published their working paper online this month, examined (3) _____, which is powered by software called large language models that can analyze and generate text. They analyzed the share of a job's tasks where GPTs, generative pre-trained transformers, and software   15
that incorporates them can reduce the time it takes to complete a task by at least 50%. Research has found that state-of-the-art GPTs excel in tasks such as translation, classification, creative writing, and generating computer code.

They found that most jobs will be changed in some form by GPTs, with 80% of workers in occupations where at least one job task can be performed more   20
quickly by generative AI. Information-processing roles, including public relations specialists, court reporters and blockchain engineers, are highly exposed, they found. (4) _____ by the technology include short-order cooks, motorcycle mechanics, and oil-and-gas roustabouts.

The real challenge, one of the authors said, is for companies, schools and   25
policy makers to help people adapt. "That's a multi-trillion dollar problem," he said, and can include, among other things, (5) _____ the technology and redesigning jobs to enhance the autonomy, wages and career prospects of many roles.

— *Based on a report on The Wall Street Journal.com on March 28, 2023* —

〈ニュース解説〉　人工知能（AI）、特に 2022 年以降に登場した「生成系」と呼ばれる AI の活用が広がりを見せる中、不安の声が増している。人間よりも高い能力を持つ AI はプロ棋士に勝利したり、画像を認識するなどこれまでも存在した。チャット GPT のような生成系 AI が、生活や仕事のあらゆる場面を支える「言葉」を巧みに操れるようになった意味が極めて大きいと言えよう。チャット GPT にも使われている大規模言語モデル（LLM）の「GPT-4」は米国の司法試験や日本の医師国家試験で合格点を取れる実力レベルとされる。LLM は「基盤モデル」とも呼ばれ、言語だけでなく画像、音声、映像など多様な情報も扱えるようにして、応用分野を広げる試みが進んでいる。AI が人類を凌駕するシンギュラリティー（技術特異点）にも関心が集まっている。

(Notes)
exposed to … （危険などに）さらされている　**generative artificial intelligence** 生成的人口知能、生成 AI　**University of Pennsylvania** ペンシルベニア大学（米ペンシルベニアに所在する私立大学）　**Open AI** オープンエーアイ、オープン AI（営利法人 OpenAI LP とその親会社である非営利法人 OpenAI Inc. からなる米国の人口ちぬの開発企業）　**ChatGPT** チャット GPT（オープン AI が 2022 年 11 月に公開した人工知能チャットボット）　**prompt** 指示　**working paper** ワーキングペーパー（予備的な科学的または技術的な論文）　**generative pre-trained transformer** 生成可能な事前学習済み変換機［今の先端人工知能を支える大規模言語モデル（LLM）の多くが用いる深層学習モデル］　**state-of-the-art** 最新式の　**classification** 分類（作業）　**generate computer code** コンピューターコードを生成する　**public relations specialist** 広報担当　**court reporter** 裁判記録官　**blockchain engineer** ブロックチェーン・エンジニア　**short-order cook** ファーストフード店の調理士　**oil-and-gas roustabout** 石油や天然ガスの掘削現場作業者　**multi-trillion dollar problem** 困難且つ多くの費用を要する問題

■問A　空所 (a) ～ (f) にそれぞれ入るべき 1 語を下記の語群から選びその番号を記せ。

iPS（人工多能性幹）細胞	→	induced pluripotent (a) cell
タッチパネル	→	touch (b)
最先端の技術	→	(c)-of-the-art technology
高速増殖炉	→	fast breeder (d)
介護施設	→	nursing-(e) facility
生活習慣病	→	lifestyle-(f) disease

1. care	2. reactor	3. related
4. screen	5. state	6. stem

■問B　空所 (a) ～ (f) にそれぞれ入るべき 1 語を下記の語群から選びその番号を記せ。

遺伝子組み換え作物	→	genetically (a) crop
太陽光発電	→	(b) power generation
地上波デジタル放送	→	digital (c) broadcasting
医療過誤	→	medical (d)
平均寿命	→	average life (e)
介助犬	→	(f) dog

1. error	2. expectancy	3. modified
4. service	5. solar	6. terrestrial

■問C　(a) ～ (h) をそれぞれ和訳せよ。

(a) biodegradable plastic
(b) room-temperature superconductivity
(c) shape-memory garments
(d) capsule endoscope
(e) optical fiber
(f) heat stroke
(g) organ transplant
(h) brain death

スポーツ

Thomas Bach "Baron Von Ripper-off"（Washington Post）
トーマス・バッハ　ぼったくり男爵（ワシントンポスト紙）
「写真提供：共同通信社」

Before you read

金権体質と商業主義が批判される IOC（国際オリンピック委員会）。その会長を務めるトーマス・バッハ氏も東京 2020 オリンピック時には、開催国を食い物にする「ぼったくり男爵」と米紙によって揶揄された。その IOC が、今度はウクライナを侵略したロシアとベラルーシの選手のオリンピック競技への参加を認める判断を下して物議を醸している。Chapter 14 では、ウクライナ問題に対する IOC と他の競技団体の対応の違いにも注目して読んでみよう。

Disk 2

IOC President Thomas Bach defends plan to include Russian and Belarusian athletes at Paris Olympics

Berlin, Germany—International Olympic Committee (IOC) President Thomas Bach has pleaded with politicians to "keep politics and sports apart" while defending the IOC's controversial plans to include Russian and Belarusian athletes at the Paris 2024 Games.

"If politics decides who can take part in a competition, then sport and athletes ⁵ become tools of politics," Bach said during an hours-long speech in German on Wednesday in Essen, Germany.

"It is then impossible for sport to transfer its uniting powers. We must be politically neutral but not apolitical. We know well that politics rules the world. We know well that our decisions have political implications and we have to include that ¹⁰ in our thinking," he added. "But we should not make the mistake of raising ourselves to referees of political disputes because we will be crushed by these political powers."

In February, the IOC reiterated its condemnation of the war in Ukraine, one year on from the beginning of the invasion, in a statement. ¹⁵

According to Reuters, Bach went on to say, "Ukraine wants, and this is a direct quote 'the total isolation of all Russians,'" as some people in the audience applauded.

"It is a dilemma for us and a completely new situation. If we exclude athletes for political reasons, we face the decline of the international sporting system," Bach said. "We feel, suffer with and understand the Ukrainian people and athletes. On the other ²⁰ hand, we have, as a global organization, a responsibility towards human rights and the Olympic Charter," he added, according to Reuters.

In January, the IOC outlined a multi-step plan for Russian and Belarusian athletes to participate at the upcoming 2024 Summer Games in Paris and the 2026 Winter Games in Milan, which was met by criticism from the United States, Canada ²⁵ and most European countries. Last month, the US and more than 30 other "like-minded" countries backed a proposed ban of Russian and Belarusian athletes from competing in international sports, according to a joint statement.

Meanwhile, Ukraine's sports minister said in January the country would not rule out boycotting the Olympics if Russian and Belarusian athletes are allowed ³⁰ to compete at Paris 2024. On Thursday, World Athletics president Sebastian Coe announced Russian and Belarusian athletes will still be excluded from World Athletics Series Events "for the foreseeable future" due to Russia's invasion of Ukraine, reaffirming the organization's March 2022 decision.

— *Based on a report on CNN.com on March 23, 2023* —

〈ニュース解説〉 2023 年 1 月、国際オリンピック委員会（IOC）は 2024 年の夏季五輪、2026 年の冬季五輪へのロシア、ベラルーシ選手の参加を、国を代表しない中立の立場を条件に認めると発表し、トーマス・バッハ同委員会会長も同委員会の決定を擁護した。この決定に対し、両国選手出場なら五輪ボイコットの可能性を表明したウクライナを初め欧州各国は反発。バッハ会長は、両国の参加は多くのスポーツで認められているとしているが、実際各競技団体においては、両国選手の大会等への参加について対応の相違が見られる。IOC の勧告に反してロシア、ベラルーシ選手の除外措置を続けるワールドアスレティックス（国際陸上競技連盟）や FIFA（国際サッカー連盟）ワールドカップとは対照的に、男子プロテニス協会（ATP）や女子テニス協会（WTA）は、「全ての国の選手を平等に大会へ参加させる」という基本原則に反するとして両国選手の大会への参加を容認している。テニスの 4 大大会（グランドスラム）では、全豪、全仏、全米の 3 つの大会は両国選手の参加を認めているが、ウィンブルドン大会のみが参加を認めず、その結果罰金措置の他に同大会でのランキングポイント付与停止と昨年大会でのポイント失効という厳しい制裁措置を ATP や WTA から課されることになった。これに対しウィンブルドン大会を主催する All England Club 側は、当初の決定を取り下げ、条件付きながら両国選手の出場を認めることとなった。

(Notes) 【※☞マークは *Useful Expressions*】

IOC　国際オリンピック委員会（各国の国内オリンピック委員会の統括組織。本部はスイスのローザンヌ）

◆ **Thomas Bach**　トーマス・バッハ［第 9 代 IOC 会長。フェンシングで、1976 年のモントリオール五輪に西ドイツ代表として出場。カネまみれの商業主義が蔓延る IOC の会長として、コロナ禍での東京五輪開催を突き進め、開催国を食い物にしているとの批判を浴び「ぼったくり男爵（Baron von Ripper-off）」と批判されることもあった］

☞◆ （L. 2）**keep ～ and ～ apart**　～と～を切り離す

◆ （L. 3-4）**Paris 2024 Games**　2024 年の夏季パリ五輪（Games は Olympic Games を省略した形）

◆ （L. 9）**apolitical**　政治に無関心な、ノンポリの（接頭辞 a- は否定を表す。例：asymmetric 非対称の）

◆ （L. 16）**Reuters**　ロイター（ロンドンに本社を置く通信社。1851 年にポール・ジュリアス・ロイターによって設立される。2007 年、カナダの情報サービス大手トムソンに買収されトムソン・ロイターの一部となる。米国のブルームバーグとともに金融情報サービスの提供でも知られる）

◆ （L. 22）**Olympic Charter**　オリンピック憲章（IOC によって採択されたオリンピックの根本原則や規則を成文化したもので、オリンピック競技大会開催の条件を規定するものでもある。6 章からなり、オリンピック・ムーヴメント、国際オリンピック委員会、国際競技連盟、国内オリンピック委員会、オリンピック競技大会、対応措置と制裁・紛争の解決等の項目がある）

◆ （L. 24-25）**2026 Winter Games in Milan**　2026 年開催の冬季ミラノ五輪（2006 年トリノで開催されて以来のイタリアでの冬季五輪開催である。英語の Milan はイタリア語では Milano）

☞◆ （L. 30）**rule out**　除外する、排除する

◆ （L. 31）**World Athletics president Sebastian Coe**　ワールドアスレティックス会長セバスティアン・コー［ワールドアスレティックスは、各国の陸上競技加盟団体を統括し、世界的陸上競技大会の運営を担う国際競技連盟。旧称の「国際陸上競技連盟（IAAF）」に代わって、2019 年 11 月から用いられている名称。日本語呼称は「世界陸連」。セバスティアン・コーは 2015 年から同連盟の会長を務める。コーは、陸上競技中距離の世界的ランナーで、モスクワ、ロサンゼルス両五輪の 1500m で連続金メダルを獲得している］

◆ （L. 32-33）**World Athletics Series Events**　ワールドアスレティックス・シリーズ大会［ワールドアスレティックス主催のいくつかある選手権大会の一つである。最も注目を集めるのが 2 年に 1 度の（biennial）世界陸上競技選手権大会（World Athletics Championships）である］

ニュースを読んで、下記の設問に答えよ。

1. 本文の内容と一致するものには T (True) を、一致しないものには F (False) を記せ。

(   ) (1) IOC President Thomas Bach takes the inseparability of politics and sports for granted.

(   ) (2) The IOC's support for the inclusion of Russian and Belarusian athletes at the 2024 Olympics reflects its long-cherished pro-Russian political stance.

(   ) (3) Ukraine disagrees with the IOC's argument against the exclusion of Russian and Belarusian athletes from the Olympic Games.

(   ) (4) The IOC's decision to include Russian and Belarusian athletes applies both to the Summer and Winter Olympics in 2024 and 2026 respectively.

(   ) (5) There is a disagreement between the United States and most European nations on whether to allow Russian and Belarusian athletes to compete in the Olympics in 2024.

(   ) (6) The unilateral approach by the US government to exclude Russia and Belarus from the Olympics does not have followers in Canada.

(   ) (7) The Ukrainians seem to be unwilling to compete with Russian and Belarusian athletes in the same international sporting events.

(   ) (8) Among international sports federations, World Athletics appears to maintain a pro-Ukraine stance in the wake of the Russian invasion of Ukraine.

2. 本文中に掲げた下記の［*Useful Expressions*］を用いて空欄に適語を記し、日本語に合う英文を完成させよ。

(1) 〈 **keep ～ apart** 〉

Islam teaches to (   ) during the worship service.

イスラム教は礼拝中男女を分けるように教えている。

(2) 〈 **rule out** 〉

Let's not (   ) that she survived the plane crash.

彼女が飛行機（墜落）事故で生き残った可能性を排除しないでおきましょう。

音声を聞き、下線部を補え。（２回録音されています。１回目はナチュラルスピード、２回目はスロースピードです。）

Natural 39
Slow 41

Japan won the World Baseball Classic on Tuesday night, downing Team USA 3-2 in the championship game at LoanDepot Park in Miami.

The game [(1)] _____ with Japan's Shohei Ohtani striking out his MLB teammate Mike Trout with a full-count slider to seal Japan's third title. Ohtani, who batted .435 and pitched to a 1.86 ERA, was also named the tournament's most valuable player.

Ohtani pitching to Trout [(2)] _____ — not only will the pair go down alongside baseball's all-time greats, but they are also Los Angeles Angels teammates.

Natural 40
Slow 42

"It was the greatest situation facing the greatest hitter, so it was great," Ohtani told ESPN. The 28-year-old added: "I've seen Japan winning, and I just [(3)] _____. I really appreciate that I was able to have the great experience. As I say, the next generation, the kids who are playing baseball, I was hoping that those people would like to play baseball. That would make me happy."

Japan won all seven games [(4)] _____ ___, its juggernaut offense scoring 53 runs in its first six contests. But Team USA pitchers limited Japan to just five hits. However, Japan was spurred by solo home runs by Munetaka Murakami and Kazuma Okamoto. Seven Japanese pitchers allowed nine US hits but Team USA was 0-for-7 [(5)] _____ _____.

— *Based on a report on CNN.com on March 22, 2023* —

〈ニュース解説〉　ワールド・ベースボール・クラシックは、メジャーリーグ・ベースボール機構（MLB）と MLB 選手会（MLBPA）から成る World Baseball Classic Inc. が主催する野球の世界一決定戦。記事にある第５回大会は、現在メジャーリーガーである大谷翔平、ダルビッシュ有、ラーズ・ヌートバー、吉田正尚等総勢 30 名を擁した日本代表侍ジャパンが、第１回、第２回大会に続いて３度目の優勝を飾る。決勝の米国戦では大谷翔平が、最後の打者で彼のチームメートのマイク・トラウトを三振に切って取り、接戦を制して優勝に導いた。

(Notes)
World Baseball Classic ワールド・ベースボール・クラシック　**LoanDepot Park** ローンデポ・パーク（米国フロリダ州マイアミにあるメジャーリーグのマイアミ・マーリンズの本拠地球場。今回の第５回大会では、準々決勝の一部、準決勝、決勝の舞台となった）　**MLB teammate Mike Trout** メジャーリーグのチームメートであるマイク・トラウト（大谷翔平とトラウトは同じメジャーリーグのチームに所属）　**ERA** 防御率〔Earned Run Average。投手の９イニングにおける平均の自責点（Earned Run。投手の責任とされる失点）で、投手が１試合で取られた点数の平均値である〕　**Los Angeles Angels** ロサンゼルス・エンジェルス（メジャーリーグのアメリカンリーグ西地区のチーム。カリフォルニア州アナハイム所在。以前はアナハイム・エンジェルスと呼ばれた）　**ESPN** イーエスピーエヌ（Entertainment and Sports Programming Network の略。アメリカのスポーツ専門チャンネル。ウォルト・ディズニー・カンパニーが主要出資者）　**juggernaut offense** 破壊力ある攻撃　**Munetaka Murakami** 村上宗隆（ヤクルトスワローズの内野手。2022 年シーズンでは、日本野球機構史上最年少の 22 歳で三冠王を達成）　**Kazuma Okamoto** 岡本和真（読売ジャイアンツの内野手で中心バッター）　**scoring position** 得点圏（シングルヒットで走者が本塁に生還できる塁のことで、２塁と３塁のこと）

■問A (a) 〜 (i) にそれぞれ対応する英語表現を下記の語群から選びその番号を記せ。

(a) 円盤投げ   (b) 砲丸投げ   (c) やり投げ

(d) ハンマー投げ   (e) 走高跳び   (f) 走幅跳び

(g) 三段跳び   (h) 棒高跳び   (i) 十種競技

1. decathlon	2. discus throw	3. hammer throw
4. high jump	5. javelin throw	6. long jump
7. pole vault	8. shot put	9. triple jump

■問B (a) 〜 (g) の体操用語にそれぞれ対応する日本語表現を下記の語群から選びその番号を記せ。

(a) balance beam   (b) floor exercise   (c) flying rings   (d) horse vault

(e) parallel bars   (f) pommel horse   (g) uneven bars

1. あん馬	2. 段違い平行棒	3. 跳馬	4. つり輪
5. 平均台	6. 平行棒	7. ゆか	

■問C (a) 〜 (j) の野球用語の説明に対応する英語を下記の語群から選びその番号を記せ。

(a) The extension of a baseball game until one team is ahead of the other at the end of an inning

(b) An out resulting from a batter getting three strikes during a time at bat

(c) Getting two players out on one play

(d) An act of deliberately hitting a baseball gently without swinging the bat so that it does not roll far into the infield

(e) A pitch that the catcher should have caught but missed, allowing runners to advance to the next base

(f) A relief pitcher who specializes in protecting a lead by getting the final outs in a close game

(g) A way of measuring a pitcher's effectiveness

(h) A pitch of a baseball that does not travel straight, as it is thrown with spin so that its path curves as it approaches the batter

(i) the sum of a player's on-base percentage and slugging percentage, which shows the player's ability both to reach base successfully and to hit for power

(j) a variation of breaking ball or a slider distinguished by a great deal of horizontal movement, i.e. more across than up and down

1. breaking ball	2. bunt	3. closer	4. double play
5. earned run average	6. extra innings	7. on-base plus slugging (OPS)	
8. passed ball	9. strikeout	10. sweeper	

THE WORLD OF ENGLISH JOURNALISM

① **News defined** ── ニュースは記者が決める？

掲載するニュースを決めるのは編集局（記者）だが、ニュースの定義には、世の中に起こっているすべてがニュースだという考えもある。しかし他方で、そのような様々な出来事からニュースにする価値あり（newsworthy）と記者が判断して選んだものがニュースだという考えもある。記者たちの中には、"We determine the news!" と公言して、ニュースは記者が作るものだと考えている人たちも多い。また、ニュースを選ぶ基準として、"what people want to know" と "what people need to know" の間のバランスを取ることも大切である。

このトピックを英文で読んでみよう。

How do you determine whether a current idea, event, or problem is news? How do you recognize it, separating swiftly the news and the non-news in what happens? How can you be sure that it will interest readers, listeners, or viewers?

To answer these questions, examine the elements common in all news. These may also be termed news values, appeals, factors, determinants, or criteria. Even if one is missing, the reporter may question whether the happening is news.

The five news elements are: (a) timeliness, (b) nearness, (c) size, (d) importance and (e) personal benefit.

② **The headline** —「見出し」の特徴

現代英文ジャーナリズムの「見出し」（headline）では、日常的に用いられない語を「見出し語」（headlinese）として使用することを避ける傾向が強い。見出しは記事の内容を簡潔明瞭に表現する必要があり、一般的に次の5つの特徴を有している。

（1）略語が多い。例えば、"GOP" と言えば "Grand Old Party" の略称で、米国共和党（Republican Party）の異名。

（2）特殊記号がある。例えば、"and" をカンマで代用したり、情報源を表すコロンがある。ヘッドラインのコロンはすべて情報源を表すものではないが、"Gunman in Manhattan kills one woman, wounds three: NYPD" とあれば、カンマは "and" に置き換えて "Gunman in Manhattan kills one woman and wounds three" となり、この情報は NYPD（New York City Police Department, ニューヨーク市警察）によってもたらされたことがわかる。

（3）冠詞や be 動詞は省略されることが多い。

（4）見出しにとどまらず、英語ニュースでは、首都名はその国や政府を表すことが多い。例えば、Washington は米国や米国政府を表す場合がよくある。もちろん首都自体のことを表す場合もあるから、文脈に注意。

（5）時制のずらしに気をつけよう。昨日起こったことでも現在形で表現。未来は to 不定詞で表現。例えば見出し語で "Government to regulate the Internet" とあれば、"The government will regulate the Internet" の意味。

このトピックを英文で読んでみよう。

The modern headline is distinguished by the fact that it says something—it makes a complete statement instead of merely characterizing. But, in addition, it speaks a language of its own. This language is not "headlinese," a perverted speech, but is merely pure English adapted to the requirements of headlining.

For one thing, the present tense is customarily used to describe past events. This usage is not something created by headline writers but is simply something borrowed from everyday speech. The present tense is employed because it is the tense of immediacy, because it is more vivid and, hence, because it makes our trial tube of toothpaste inviting to the prospective buyer.

Another characteristic, which is more obvious to the ordinary reader, is the omission of non-essential words, chiefly articles. This practice has a tendency to give the headline telegraphic speed and, hence, to make it more vivid.

Still another characteristic of headline language is the use of short words, mainly of Anglo-Saxon derivation. And, here again, the space requirement is the commanding factor.

③ The inverted pyramid ― 逆ピラミッドとは

英文のニュースの大半は、ハード・ニュース（hard news）と呼ばれ、経済・政治・犯罪・事故・災害などに関連して日々起こる重要な出来事をスピーディーかつ簡潔に読者に伝える内容となっている。新聞の読者、テレビやラジオの視聴者、さらにはインターネットの利用者にとって時間は最も貴重な資源であり、多くの人たちは限られた時間内に最大限の情報を入手する必要に迫られている。こうしたニーズに対応するために考案されたのが逆ピラミッド型と呼ばれるニュースの構成であり、Chapter 6 で紹介するフィーチャー・ニュース（feature news）の構成と対比される。

このトピックを英文で読んでみよう。

This news writing format summarizes the most important facts at the very start of the story. It may seem like an obvious idea to us nowadays—getting right to the point when you start a story—but it did not occur to most reporters until midway through the 19th century. What changed? Sentences got shorter. Writing got tighter. And reporters developed a formula for compressing the most newsworthy facts—the who, what, when, where, why—into the opening paragraphs of a story. That formula lives on today. It is known as the inverted pyramid.

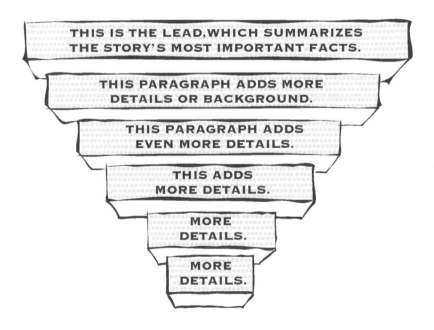

THIS IS THE LEAD, WHICH SUMMARIZES THE STORY'S MOST IMPORTANT FACTS.

THIS PARAGRAPH ADDS MORE DETAILS OR BACKGROUND.

THIS PARAGRAPH ADDS EVEN MORE DETAILS.

THIS ADDS MORE DETAILS.

MORE DETAILS.

MORE DETAILS.

④ **The lead** ― リードの役割

すべてのニュースがこの形をとるわけではないが、特に "hard news" は、リードと呼ばれる導入部でニュースの要約を伝えるのが普通である。一般に five W's and one H のすべての要素が、最初の1～2の段落に凝縮される。「lead（リード）」は「headline（見出し）」のすぐ後に書かれ、リードの後に続くのが「body（本文）」である。ヘッドラインはスペース上の問題もあり記事の内容を正確に伝えきれないこともあるが、リードは記事の内容を冒頭で要約して、読者に端的に伝える。

このトピックを英文で読んでみよう。

A news story has two main parts: a lead and a body.

Usually the lead is the opening paragraph but may include the second and third paragraphs as well. It is the essence of the news as presented in summary form at the beginning of the story.

A typical lead is:

Telephone wires leading into 15 dwellings were cut yesterday afternoon, apparently by vandals, interrupting service for 25 users.

Leads have many constructions and patterns of their own. Generally, however, they seek to answer six questions about the news—Who? What? When? Where? Why? and How?

The body of the story is all the rest beyond the lead, no matter whether the remainder is three or 30 paragraphs long. The arrangement of the body often follows logically from the lead, but it, too, must be planned.

FBI search a house where Faisal Shahzad lived in Bridgeport, Conn., Tuesday, May 4, 2010.

⑤ **Beyond the basic news lead** ― 異なるスタイルのリード

社会問題や面白そうな人物を扱った記事等、解説的要素が大きく入り込む記事においては、前章で触れたような事実だけを並べた要約的なリードで記事を書き始めたのでは何とも味気ない。すべてのニュースが時宜を得たものであるとは限らない。昨日今日のニュースのように即時性が要求されるニュースでない場合は、もっと生き生きしたクリエイティヴで掘り下げた、場合によっては楽しく人をわくわくさせる記事の書き方が求められる。

このトピックを英文で読んでみよう。

It is not mandatory to begin every story with a roundup of essential facts. For most breaking news events, you need leads that are quick, factual, and concise. You need leads that summarize the who-what-when-where-why. But not every story is a timely news event. Some stories explore social issues. Some profile interesting people. And for those, a basic news lead may be too dull and dry. You may need something livelier, snappier, more creative, a lead that does not just summarize but amuses, astonishes, and intrigues.

NEWS MEDIA IN THE WORLD

通信社　News Agencies (1)

✓ "news agency" や "news service" と呼ばれる「通信社」は、独自の取材陣又は国内外の報道機関などと連携し、作成したニュース記事を写真やビデオ映像などとともに新聞社、放送社へ配信する組織。膨大な取材ネットワークが必要なため、単独の新聞社等では対応が困難なことから、報道機関が共同して通信社を設ける非営利型の組合組織も多い。

⑥ The world of features ― フィーチャー・ニュースの世界

"feature news"（フィーチャー・ニュース）は日本語では「特集記事」や「読み物」などと訳される。また、"hard news" と対比して "soft news" と呼ばれることもある。日本を台風が直撃し、その当日あるいは翌日、その被害を報じれば "hard news" である。その後、台風で家を失った住民の生活に焦点を当てて報じれば "feature news" となる。新聞などで報じられるニュースの大半は "hard news" であるが、報道のスピードという点で新聞はインターネットに遅れを取らざるを得ず、インターネットの普及に伴い、新聞の記事に占める "feature news" の割合が増加傾向にあるとの指摘もある。

このトピックを英文で読んでみよう。

Some old-timers treat news and features as if they are two separate things. News, they insist, is the factual reporting of serious events, while features involve all that other, nonessential stuff. It is not that simple, though. Journalists often find it difficult to distinguish between news and features. News stories usually focus on events that are timely and public: government activity, crime, disasters. Feature stories often focus on issues that are less timely and more personal: trends, relationships, entertainment. News stories tell you what happened; feature stories offer you advice, explore ideas, and make you laugh and cry.

NEWS MEDIA IN THE WORLD

通信社　News Agencies (2)

✓　世界最初の近代的通信社は 1835 年フランスに生まれたアバスを母体とする AFP 通信（Agence France-Presse）。19 世紀半ばに創立の英国のロイター通信（Reuters）も業界の老舗。同時期に米国で設立された AP 通信（Associated Press）は組合型通信社の最大手。両社とも全世界に取材網を持ち、近時は経済ニュースにも力を入れる。経済情報の分野では Bloomberg の影響力も侮れない。

⑦ **From print to the Web** ― 紙媒体からウェブの重層的構造へ

新聞協会の調査によると、日本における日刊紙発行部数（一般紙とスポーツ紙の双方を含む。朝刊・夕刊セットは 1 部と計上）は 1999 年の約 5,376 万部から 2022 年には約 3,678 万部へと減少傾向にある。今後新聞などの紙媒体が消滅してしまうことはないだろうが、ウェブ・ニュース（オンライン・ニュース）には、新聞にはない魅力がある。すなわち、ウェブ・ニュースは様々なメディアの融合体で、新聞のようにニュースを横並びに読むのではなく、ワン・クリックで様々なメディアや情報に重層的にアクセスすることができる。

このトピックを英文で読んでみよう。

Print journalism will not go extinct. But it will become increasingly difficult to compete against the allure of digital media, where editors can combine text, photos, audio, video, animated graphics, interactive chat, and much more. Online media offer readers more variety. Stories, images, and digital extras can be linked together in layers, with related options just a click away. Instead of arranging stories side by side, the way traditional newspapers do, online news sites link related topics in layers that allow readers to roam from story to story.

NEWS MEDIA IN THE WORLD

通信社　News Agencies (3)

✔ ロシア国営のイタル・タス通信（ITAR-TASS）は、ソビエト連邦時代の 1925 年に誕生したタス通信（TASS）が母体。冷戦期は、政府の公式情報発信機関だったが、ソビエト崩壊後、規模を縮小。中国の新華社通信 "Xinhua News Agency" も国営で中国政府及び共産党の公式見解を報道。政治問題などについて、報道内容や時間的対応状況から、政府の意向や内部事情などを占うことも多い。

⑧ **Broadcast news** ― 放送ニュースの特質

放送ニュースは、テレビやラジオの映像や音声を通じて視聴者の感情に訴えることができ、現実を生で伝える力がある。視聴者も面倒な記事を読む煩わしさから解放され、頭を使うことが少なくて済むから大人気。新聞や雑誌といった紙媒体のようなニュースの深みや掘り下げはないが、視聴者へのアピール度や即時性（immediacy）といった面では軍配が上がる。なお、最近では従来のテレビやラジオに加えて、インターネットで聴けるネット・ラジオ、携帯音楽プレイヤーに音声データ・ファイルとして配信される "Podcast"（ポッドキャスト）や携帯電話で視聴できる "One-Seg television"（ワンセグ・テレビ）等、放送ニュースのメディアも実に多様化してきている。

このトピックを英文で読んでみよう。

TV and radio journalism is neither better nor worse than print journalism. It is just different. Each form of media has strengths and weaknesses. Print journalism provides a level of depth, context and sheer information that television and radio newscasts can not supply. Broadcast journalism, through the power of dramatic video and engaging audio, offers an emotional appeal, realism and immediacy that printed stories can not match. Watching or listening to a news broadcast generally requires less intellectual effort than reading a complex news story in a newspaper.

NEWS MEDIA IN THE WORLD

通信社　News Agencies (4)

✔ 日本の共同通信社（Kyodo News Service）と時事通信社（JIJI Press）は第 2 次大戦中の国策通信社・同盟通信社が 1945 年に分割されて出来た。中央、地方の新聞や放送へのニュース記事配信とともに、行政機関や民間会社への情報提供サービスを行っている。近時、アジアを中心に英語による国際的な発信活動にも力を入れている。

⑨ **Radio news reporting** ― ラジオ・ニュースの難しさ

テレビのような映像がなく、新聞・雑誌のように長々と叙述できないのがラジオのニュース。ラジオの聞き手は何か他のことをしながらラジオ・ニュースを聞いている。そうなると、ニュースも簡潔、そして聞き手の注意を一発で喚起する書き方が要求される。記者には、ニュースを30秒でまとめる技術が求められる。"actuality" または "sound bite"（ニュースで繰り返し放送される録音テープからの抜粋）、"natural sound" または "ambient sound"（周囲の様子を伝えるような音声や環境音）、"lead-in"（ニュース番組の導入部分）等はラジオニュース関連の専門用語。テレビ・ニュースの用語と共通するものも多い。最近はインターネットで聞けるラジオサイトも増え、世界中のラジオ放送を無料で聞くことが出来る。ホームページでは豊富な英文記事の他に、ラジオ・ニュースも聴取できる。BBC World Service（英）、NPR（米）、ABC Radio National（豪）等にアクセスしてオンライン・ラジオ・ニュースを聴いてみよう。

このトピックを英文で読んでみよう。

Radio journalism may be the most challenging form of news reporting. You can not rely on graphics and images as TV reporters do. You can not write long, descriptive sentences and stories as print reporters do. When people are listening to your story on the radio, they are doing it while they dodge traffic, talk on their cellphone, and do their makeup. So radio news writing needs to be as direct and attention-grabbing as possible. Word economy is the key. The best radio reporting is snappy yet eloquent, conversational yet concise, friendly yet authoritative. Most stories at most stations require their reporters to boil everything down to its 30-second essence.

⑩ **Media convergence** ― メディアの融合化への流れ

昨今のジャーナリズムは、マルチメディアを駆使して情報を伝達する。1つのことを伝えるにも、写真、オーディオ、ビデオ（動画）、テキスト（文字データ）というようにあらゆる媒体を使って、より理想に近い情報を作り出し伝達することが出来るのがメディア融合の強みである。

このトピックを英文で読んでみよう。

Suppose you decided to profile Ludwig van Gogh, a brilliant painter and composer. Which medium, or media, would produce the best story? To display his paintings, you would use photographs. To present his music, you would use audio recordings. To show him at work—conducting an orchestra or painting—you would use video footage. To explain the meaning and impact of his art, you would use text. In short, to create the ideal profile, you would need multimedia. Cross-platform journalism, media convergence—whatever you call it, it is an idea whose time has finally come.

NEWS MEDIA IN THE WORLD

新聞社 Newspapers (1)

✔ 英国では、庶民を読者とする大衆紙には昔からタブロイド判（tabloid）が多いが、これまで大判（broadsheet）で出されていた高級紙 *Times* や *Guardian* も判型をタブロイド判に変えつつある。2015 年以降日本経済新聞傘下にある高級経済紙 *Financial Times*（略称 FT）は大判でピンク色の用紙が特徴。近年経費削減等の理由から紙面の縮小が流行で、*Guardian* やフランスの *Le Monde* など、大判とタブロイド判の中間の大きさのベルリーナ判（Berliner format）を採用する新聞もあった。*Guardian* は、その後 2018 年に判型をベルリーナ判からタブロイド判に変更し、*Times* と並び英国高級紙のタブロイド判化として話題となった。

①～⑩ではニュースの定義から始めて、ニュースの種類、ニュースの構成要素と組み立て方といったポイントを概観すると共に、紙媒体のニュース、オンラインニュース、映像や音声で伝えるニュースの特質と、これらのニュースの融合化の流れを紹介した。⑪～⑮ではジャーナリストがひとつひとつの表現や文章を書く上で留意すべき5つの重要点を検討する。

⑪ Passive verbs ― 受身の動詞

即時性や解り易さを旨とする英文ジャーナリズムの世界では、より直接的で、迫力のある文章を作るため、能動態を用い、動詞の受身用法（be ＋過去分詞）は避けるべき、というのが常識。

受身用法は、

➢ 主張内容があいまいになり、文章にインパクトがなくなる
➢ 主語や主体がわかりにくく、誰の意見か不明で無責任な内容になりやすい
➢ There is ～や There are ～を使う表現は読者に迂遠で慇懃な感じを与える
➢ 能動態より be 動詞と動作主を示す by が増えることで文章が長くなる

などのデメリットがある。

パンチのあるニュース記事を書くためには、力強く、直接的でイメージのわく動詞を選ぶ事も大切だ。

このトピックを英文で読んでみよう。

There is a problem many reporters struggle with. The sentences that are written by them are passive. Their phrasing is made awkward because of this, and—wait! *Stop!*

Let's rewrite that paragraph to make it less *passive*:

Many reporters struggle because they write passive sentences. This makes their phrasing awkward.

See the difference? We have strengthened our syntax by starting sentences with their subjects. We have eliminated that clunky phrase *there is*. And we have replaced the verb *to be* (words such as *is* and *are*), with stronger verbs.

You do not have to be a grammar geek to see our point here. Make your sentences *emphatic*. Avoid weak, flabby verbs.

NEWS MEDIA IN THE WORLD

新聞社 Newspapers (2)

✓ 米国の新聞は発行部数の少ない地域紙が主流。リベラルな高級紙といわれる *New York Times* や *Washington Post*、*Los Angeles Times* も地方紙だ。米国では、地方紙で研鑽を積んだ記者が高級紙や全国放送の記者に採用されるのが一般的。1980 年代に全米を対象に創刊された *USA Today* も各地域のニュースをフォロー。経済紙の *Wall Street Journal*（略称 WSJ）は、経済通信社の Dow Jones の所有。保守的論調で知られる。

⑫ **Redundancy** — 冗長な文章を避ける

不必要な語や表現を使用すると文章は冗長になる。例えば、形容詞と名詞の組み合わせでは、名詞にその形容詞の意味がもとから含まれている場合にその表現は冗長となる。副詞と動詞の組み合わせにおいても、動詞がその副詞の意味を持つ場合に同様の問題が発生する。ニュースルームでは、記者が作成したニュース原稿は編集デスクに送られ文体や内容のチェックを受けた後、報道される。

このトピックを英文で読んでみよう。

Sometimes it is not so obvious that you are using unnecessary words and phrases. Why say that someone is *currently* president of the club? Or that the game is *scheduled for* Friday night? Or that the victims were burned *in the flames*?

Those italicized words add bulk, but no extra meaning. Just as bad are phrases such as these, which are simply doublespeak:

grateful thanks	true fact	personal opinion
all-time record	end result	serious danger
totally destroyed	very unique	first time ever

Be on the lookout for unnecessary modifiers that *sound* logical but add nothing. Eliminate waste. Edit yourself ruthlessly. As Mark Twain once advised: "When in doubt, strike it out."

NEWS MEDIA IN THE WORLD

新聞社 Newspapers (3)

✓ ロシアのプラウダ（*Pravda*）、中国の人民日報（*People's Daily*）はいずれも両国共産党の機関紙として出発。ソビエト崩壊や中国の近代化により情報発信の多様化が進んだが、報道活動に一定の制限がある中国では政府の意向を窺うメディアとして依然重要。アジアでは、シンガポールの英字紙 *Straits Times* や華字紙の『聯合早報』、タイの英字紙 *Nation*、日本の英字紙 *Japan Times* 等がある。FT や WSJ のアジア版、*New York Times* の世界版である *International New York Times*（かつての *International Herald Tribune*）等が各地で印刷発行されている。

⑬ **Long, long, long wordy sentences** ― 長い、長い、長い冗漫な文体

小説や論説等でも長くて冗長な文章は敬遠される今日である。ましてや事件や出来事の報道を行うハード・ニュースの記事は正確で簡潔（precise and concise）が生命線。即時報道を目的としないフィーチャー・ニュース、即ち特集記事や読み物においてさえも、長くて取り留めのない文体はニュース記事では避けるべきである。一昔前までは英文で論理を展開する上では理想的な句や節と考えられていた表現方法、或いは過度な丁寧表現のように相手の立場に配慮した言い回しは、ストレートさが欠ける点で逆に文章内容をより複雑にして今日の読者に分かりにくくしている場合もある。ニュース英語のみならずビジネス英語でも同じような状況に遭遇するが、文章は説明口調ではなく簡潔さを保つことによってかえって伝える側の意図が迅速に且つ正確に読者に伝わることはしばしば指摘される。下の英文は、冗漫な文の典型例であるが、冗長な文体を避けるという本課の主旨からすると真逆の書き方でそのような文体を戒めているところが面白い。文章が lengthy 或いは wordy であるということは、退屈な（tedious）文章であることと表裏一体であることを忘れるべきではない。下の英文でも分かるように、文を長くするには様々な表現や方法があるが、文を短く正確に書くことは比較的難しい。

このトピックを英文で読んでみよう。

It should be pointed out that many writers, in order to make themselves sound much more profound and scholarly than perhaps they actually are, use flabby, inflated wording such as "it should be pointed out" and "in order to" and "perhaps"—which we just did ourselves, in fact, earlier in this sentence—in addition to piling up clauses (some using dashes such as those a few words back) or parentheses, such as those in the line above, not to mention semicolons, which often suggest that the writer wants to end the sentence but just cannot bring himself to actually type a period; nonetheless, today's busy readers are too impatient to tolerate the sort of 18th-century pomposity wherein writers, so in love with the sound of their own voices, just go on and on and on and on...

NEWS MEDIA IN THE WORLD

放送 Broadcasting (1)

✓ 20世紀初頭のラジオ、その後のテレビの発達を受け、放送ニュースは即時性と広域性を武器に成長。国際ニュース放送の老舗は英国 BBC（British Broadcasting Corporation）。世界中に広がる取材網を駆使、ラジオの World Service やテレビの BBC World で他をリードしてきた。米国 VOA（Voice of America）は米国国務省の対外宣伝部門として発足。冷戦時代には東側への西側意見の伝達役を担ったが、現在は、世界的なニュース専門機関の地位を確立している。

⑭ **Jargon and journalese** ─ 専門用語とジャーナリズム調の文体

ニュースにとって最も重要なことは「分かりやすい」ことだ。誰もが忙しい現代、基本的に「読み捨て」される新聞記事は誰が読んでもきちんと内容が伝わること、いちいち読み返さなくても分かることが非常に重要だからである。英語の新聞の場合でも、難解な言葉や表現を避け、単語そのものもできるだけわかりやすい short words を用いる。例えば purchase → buy、attempt → try、anticipate → expect、utilize → use、request → ask、obtain → get などである。しかし、時に新聞記事は陳腐で大げさなジャーナリズム的表現に陥りがちであることも事実だ。

このトピックを英文で読んでみよう。

Bureaucrats love to use words like *utilize*, *finalize*, and *structured*. Cops like to say suspects are *apprehended* and *incarcerated*. And if you are a campus spokesman, why would you want to say "*the school can't afford to pay raises*" when you could say "*the salary scale revision will adversely affect the university's financial stability*"?

Good reporters relentlessly strive to filter out bloated, convoluted jargon and officialese. And those who do not should be *redirected*, *transitioned*, or *subject to personnel surplus reduction* (i.e., fired).

But reporters often lapse into "journalese" without realizing it. Journalese, as veteran editor Joe Grimm puts it, is the peculiar language that newspapers have evolved that reads like this:

Negotiators yesterday, in an eleventh-hour decision following marathon talks, hammered out an agreement on a key wage provision they earlier had rejected.

That's not as bad as bureaucratic gobbledygook. But it is still a problem, because it is still full of clichés.

NEWS MEDIA IN THE WORLD

放送 Broadcasting (2)

✓ 放送産業の故郷米国では、ラジオ放送についで、1940 年代には商業テレビ放送が開始。CBS（Columbia Broadcasting System）、NBC（National Broadcasting Company）、ABC（American Broadcasting Company）の 3 大ネットワーク時代が続いたが、現在では FOX を含め 4 大ネットワークと呼ばれることもある。さらに地上波放送に飽き足らない視聴者のニーズに応える形でケーブルテレビが急拡大。80 年代には CNN（Cable News Network）が衛星放送による世界初のニュース専門テレビ局として誕生。衛星放送が東側住民へ情報を提供し、冷戦終結に貢献したという評価もある。

⑮ Clichés（クリシェ）― 使い古された常套句

クリシェ（cliché）はフランス語語源で、「使い古され手垢がついてしまった陳腐な常套句」を意味する。元々は目新しくインパクトのある表現だったが、あまりにも使われすぎたため陳腐化してしまった比喩、イディオム、キャッチフレーズ、（聖書、文学作品、映画のセリフ等からの）引用、ことわざ、外来語、流行語などが含まれる。ライターの頭の中にはクリシェが定着してしまっているので、ニュースを書く際にも安易に、あるいは、無意識にクリシェを使ってしまいがちである。しかし、クリシェの使用は文を空疎で魅力のないものにしてしまう危険性があるので、できるだけ回避するのが望ましいとされている。*The New York Times Manual of Style and Usage* でも、「クリシェを用いる場合にはそれらを用いることに妥当性があるか否か（whether their use can be justified）を慎重に検討すべきだが、大抵の場合、その使用に妥当性はない」としている。クリシェと思われる表現をニュースの中で使おうとする場合には、その適切性・新鮮味をきちんと吟味することが必須である。*News Reporting and Writing*（Menche, 1987）によると、英国の作家でジャーナリストでもある George Orwell（ジョージ・オウェル）も、「印刷物で見慣れた表現を使用する時には常に慎重に」とライターに警告している。

このトピックを英文で読んでみよう。

Beyond the shadow of a doubt, you should work 24/7 to avoid clichés like the plague. Hel-*lo*? It's a no-brainer. Go ahead—make my day.

Tired, worn-out clichés instantly lower the IQ of your writing. So do corny newswriting clichés (a form of journalese) like these:

> The *close-knit community* was *shaken by the tragedy*.
>
> *Tempers flared over a laundry list of complaints*.
>
> The *embattled mayor* is *cautiously optimistic*, but *troubled youths* face an *uncertain future* sparked by *massive blasts* in *bullet-riddled, shark-infested waters*.
>
> So *now begins the heartbreaking task of cleaning up*.

Yes, clichés *can* come in handy. And yes, a skilled writer can use them in clever ways. Once in a blue moon.

NEWS MEDIA IN THE WORLD

放送 Broadcasting (3)

✓ CNN の成功を受け、90 年代以降ニュース専門チャンネルが続々登場。米国では、映像産業から派生した米国 FOX ニュースが参入。中東カタールにはアル・ジャジーラ（Al Jazeera）が誕生。インターネットとの融合による映像情報サービスの拡大を背景に、既存ニュース・メディアも含めた世界大のメディアミックス競争が進行中だ。

参考文献

R.E. Garst & T.M. Bernstein, *Headlines and Deadlines*, Columbia University Press (1963)

L.A. Campbell & R.E. Wolseley, *How to Report and Write the News*, Prentice-Hall (1961)

Tim Harrower, *Inside Reporting*, McGraw-Hill (2009)

The Missouri Group, *News Reporting and Writing*, Bedford / St Martins (2010)

William E. Blundell, *The Art and Craft of Feature Writing based on The Wall Street Journal Guide*, Plume (1988)

Darrell Christian, *The Associated Press Stylebook 2010 and Briefing on Media Law*, Associated Press (2010)

Rene J. Cappon, *The Associated Press Guide to News Writing*, 3rd ed., ARCO (2005),

Bill Kovach & Tom Rosenstiel, *The Elements of Journalism*, Three Rivers Press (2007)

Allan M. Siegal and William G. Connolly, *The New York Times Manual of Style and Usage*, Three Rivers Press (1999)

Paul R. Martin, (2002), *The Wall Street Journal Essential Guide to Business Style and Usage*, Free Press (2002)

Thomas W. Lippman, *The Washington Post Desk-Book on Style*, 2nd ed., McGraw-Hill (1989)

Brian S. Brooks & James L. Pinson, *Working with Words*, 2nd ed., St. Martin,s Press (1993)

Carole Rich, *Writing and Reporting News*, 5th ed., Thomson Wadsworth (2002)

藤井章雄, 『放送ニュース英語 音を読む』, 朝日出版社（1983）

藤井章雄, 『ニュース英語がわかる本』, PHP 研究所（1992）

藤井章雄, 『ニュース英語の翻訳プロセス』, 早稲田大学出版部（1996）

藤井章雄, 『放送ニュース英語の体系』, 早稲田大学出版部（2004）

日本英語コミュニケーション学会紀要 第7巻（1998）, 8巻（1999）, 11巻（2002）, 12巻（2003）, 13巻（2004）, 15巻（2006）, 17巻（2008）, 18巻（2009）, 19巻（2010）, 20巻（2011）, 21巻（2012）, 22巻（2013）

時事英語の総合演習

― 2024 年度版 ―

| 検印省略 | © 2024年1月31日　第1版発行 |

編著者	堀江　洋文
	小西　和久
	宮崎　修二
	内野　泰子

発行者　　　　　　　小川　洋一郎

発行所　　　　　　株式会社　朝 日 出 版 社
101-0065　東京都千代田区西神田 3-3-5
電話　東京 (03)3239-0271
FAX　東京 (03)3239-0479
e-mail　text-e@asahipress.com
振替口座　00140-2-46008
組版／製版・信毎書籍印刷株式会社

本書の一部あるいは全部を無断で複写複製（撮影・デジタル化を含む）及び転載することは、法律上で認められた場合を除き、禁じられています。
乱丁・落丁はお取り替えいたします。

ISBN 978-4-255-15714-6　C 1082

ちょっと手ごわい、でも効果絶大！
最強のリスニング強化マガジン

 **ENGLISH EXPRESS**

音声ダウンロード付き　毎月6日発売　定価1,375円（本体1,250円＋税10%）※2023年10月からの新定価

定期購読をお申し込みの方には
本誌1号分無料ほか、特典多数。
詳しくは下記ホームページへ。

英語が楽しく続けられる！

重大事件から日常のおもしろネタ、
スターや著名人のインタビューなど、
CNNの多彩なニュースを
生の音声とともにお届けします。
3段階ステップアップ方式で
初めて学習する方も安心。
どなたでも楽しく続けられて
実践的な英語力が身につきます。

資格試験の強い味方！

ニュース英語に慣れれば、TOEIC®テストや英検の
リスニング問題も楽に聞き取れるようになります。

CNN ENGLISH EXPRESS ホームページ

英語学習に役立つコンテンツが満載！

[本誌のホームページ] https://ee.asahipress.com/
[編集部のTwitter] https://twitter.com/asahipress_ee

朝日出版社 〒101-0065 東京都千代田区西神田 3-3-5　TEL 03-3263-3321